CANDY STROTHER DEVORE MITCHELL

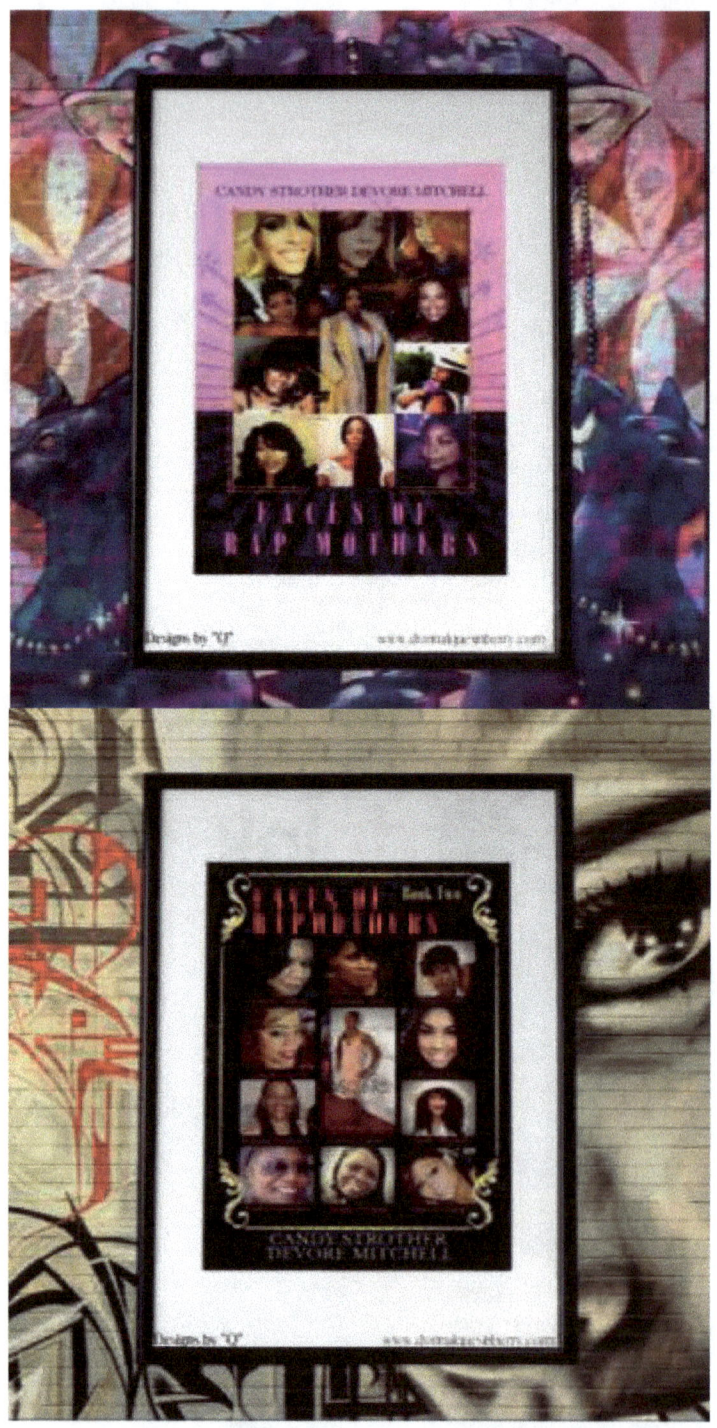

FACES OF RAP MOTHERS

Beat Deep Books | *Donna*Ink Publications, L.L.C.

United States of America

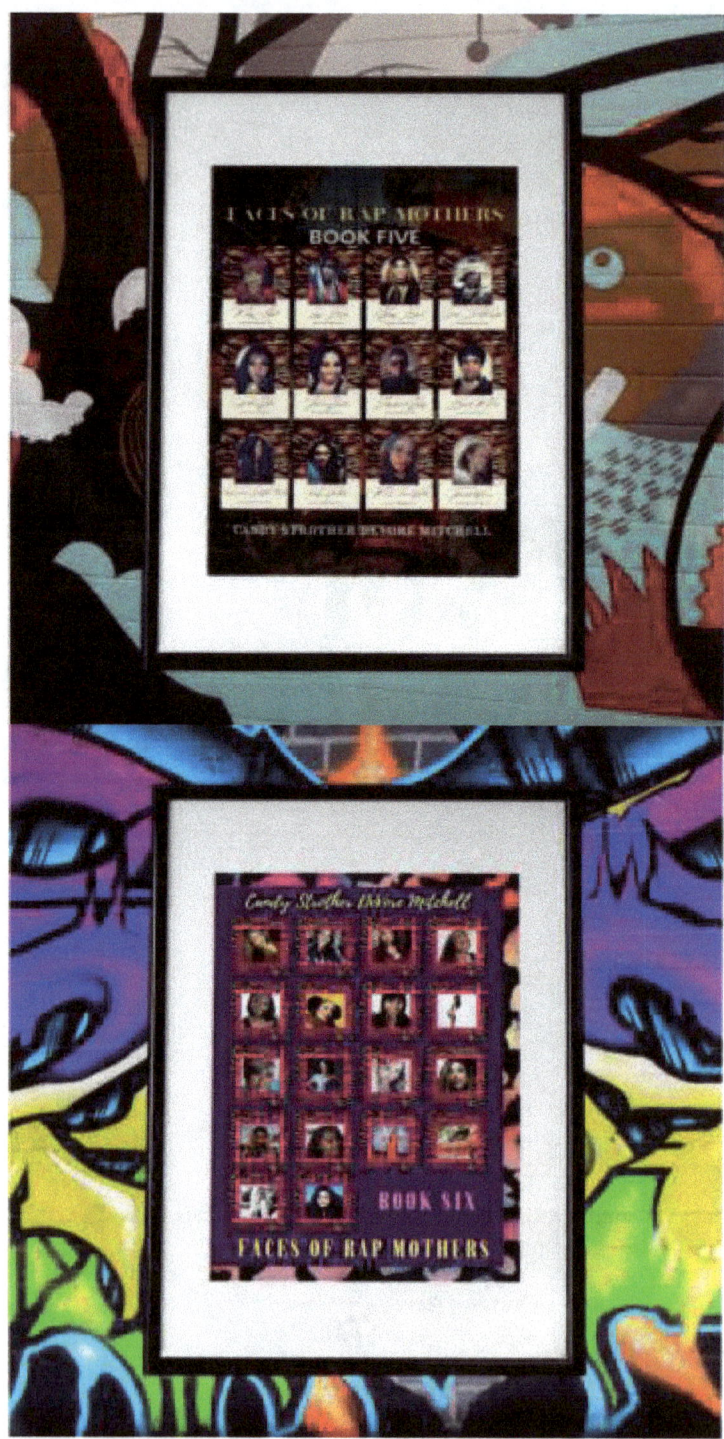

FACES OF RAP MOTHERS

by
**CANDY STROTHER
DEVORE MITCHELL**

CANDY STROTHER DEVORE MITCHELL

Beat Deep Books Imprint
An imprint of DonnaInk Publications, L.L.C.
17611 Aquasco Road
Brandywine, MD 20613

Copyright © 2021 by Candy Strother DeVore Mitchell.

DonnaInk Publications supports copyright, which creates a perceptive ethos, inspires innovation of the written word, nurtures unique vision, and promotes free speech. **DonnaInk Publications** appreciates purchase of an authorized edition of this book and copyright law compliance in not reproducing, scanning, or distributing any part of this book without prior written permission. This is a represented title, merchandise and series any/all titles sharing the *Faces of Rap Mothers*™ or *Rap Mothers*©®™ *Save the Day* are under copyright through Beat Deep Books and Little Buggy Productions Imprints of **DonnaInk**.
Library of Congress Cataloging-in-Publication.
Mitchell, Candy Strother DeVore, author. Quesinberry, Donna, ghostwriter w/credit.
Title: Faces of Rap Mothers Book Four™ / Candy Strother DeVore Mitchell.
270 p. cm.
Subjects: BIO004000-BIOGRAPHY & AUTOBIOGRAPHY/Music; BIO032000 -BIOGRAPHY & AUTOBIOGRAPHY / Social Activists; BIO022000 BIOGRAPHY & AUTOBIOGRAPHY / Women; MUS031000-MUSIC / Genres & Styles / Rap & Hip Hop; MUSIC / Genres & Styles / Rhythm & Blues see Genres & Styles / Soul & R 'n B; SOC028000 SOCIAL SCIENCE / Women's Studies; SOC001000 SOCIAL SCIENCE / Ethnic Studies / African American Studies.
Identifiers: ISBN – 13 – 9798770384260 – (alk. b/w paper).

Printed in the United States of America
First Edition: 12 11 10 9 8 7 6 5 4 3 1 Edition; 2021. All Rights Reserved.

PUBLISHER'S NOTE: This book is autobiographical fiction. References to real people, events, establishments, organizations, or locales are intended to provide a sense of authenticity and are used in a documented fashion. Views and opinions expressed are the authors. The author does not assume or claim liability if any loss, damage, or disruption is caused by errors or omissions, except where such errors or omissions result from negligence, accident, or any other cause – this work is for entertainment purposes of the author. All characters, and incidents and dialogue, are drawn from the author and contributor memory. Contributors provide stories and images to the author for discretionary use and hold author, ghostwriter, and publisher indemnified having no liability toward their work and having stated no need for formal permissions requirement when publisher requested permissions, which are normally required. No part of this book can be reproduced in any manner, including the cover, by contributors, author, their business concerns, and/or the public without written permission from the publisher. Brief quotations in critical articles and reviews are enabled. Additionally, fact-checking of names and locations, alter from author, contributors, and available resources and may not represent actual history – these are subject to reader interpretation. Misspellings based on past-or-present associations are the author's responsibility. Fact checking for correct spellings were attempted; however, many parties have multiple names and/or changed names without formal documentation available within the wherewithal of title representation by the publisher or author regarding historical fact-finding and the time required to do so. This book is for entertainment.

For more information contact:
DonnaInk Publications, L.L.C.

www.donnaink.shop | www.facesofrapmothers.com | www.donnalquesinberry.com

DonnaInk Publications, L.L.C. | Beat Deep Books Copyright Protected

ACCOLADES

NOTES FROM INDUSTRY AND REVIEWS

AWARDS:

Soul Central Magazine's Mark Rowe nominated Faces of Rap Mothers, Second Edition - Book One.

"The Most Entertaining Hip-Hop Book in 2019."

CANDY STROTHER DEVORE MITCHELL

REVIEWS:

*Amazing book, amazing author! A must read!
Ms. Bonnie Williams – Late*

Stanley "Tookie" Williams Wife

"... I love learning about the talent and new talent that has come out of the hip hop community. Everybody will love this book ... reminds me of the Behind the Music ... gives a glimpse of the portrayals and truths about hip hop ...Cheyenne – Rap Artist

OTHER BOOKS
BY CANDY STROTHER DEVORE MITCHELL

Rap Mothers®™© Save The Day Series

Book One - 02/13/20
Book Two – 11/30/21
Book Three – 11/15/25
Book Four –TBA
Book Five – TBA
Book Six – TBA
Book Seven – TBA
Book Eight – TBA
Book Nine – TBA
Book Ten – TBA

Faces of Rap Mothers®™© Book Series

Faces of Rap Mothers™ - Book One – 02/13/20
Faces of Rap Mothers™ - Book Two – 10/01/20
Faces of Rap Mothers™ - Book Three – 12/15/20
Faces of Rap Mothers™ - Book Four – 10/31/21
Faces of Rap Mothers™ - Book Five – 03/15/26

*Donna*Ink Publications, L.L.C. | Beat Deep Books Copyright Protected

CANDY STROTHER DEVORE MITCHELL

Faces of Rap Mothers™ - Book Six – TBA
Faces of Rap Mothers™ - Book Seven – TBA
Faces of Rap Mothers™ - Book Eight – TBA
Faces of Rap Mothers™ - Book Nine – TBA
Faces of Rap Mothers™ - Book Ten – TBA

Faces of Rap Mothers®™© *Fathers Editions*

Book One – 11/25/21
Book Two – TBA
Book Three – TBA
Book Four – TBA
Book Five – TBA
Book Six – TBA
Book Eight – TBA
Book Nine – TBA
Book Ten – TBA

Faces of Rap Mothers®™© *Presents . . .*

Group X - Book One – 11/07/21
Curvy Queens of Dallas - Book Two – 03/07/22
Book Three – TBA
Book Four – TBA
Book Five – TBA
Book Six – TBA
Book Seven – TBA
Book Eight – TBA
Book Nine – TBA
Book Ten – TBA

*Donna*Ink Publications, L.L.C. | Beat Deep Books Copyright Protected

TABLE OF CONTENTS
SHAPE OF THINGS TO COME

ACCOLADES	xi
NOTES FROM	xi
INDUSTRY AND REVIEWS	xi
OTHER BOOKS	xiii
BY CANDY STROTHER	xiii
DEVORE MITCHELL	xiii
TABLE OF CONTENTS	xv
SHAPE OF THINGS TO COME	xv
EPIGRAPH	xix
MOSS DEF	xix
FOREWORD	xxi
JEFFREY	xxi
COLLINS	xxi
ACKNOWLEDGEMENTS	xxv
CANDY STROTHER	xxv
DEVORE MITCHELL	xxv

DonnaInk Publications, L.L.C. | Beat Deep Books Copyright Protected

INTRODUCTION xxix
MS. DONNA L. xxix
QUESINBERRY xxix

CHAPTER ONE 1
CANDY STROTHER 1
DEVORE MITCHELL 1

CHAPTER TWO 25
ANTONETTE 29
AMES 29

CHAPTER THREE 41
DIANNA 41
BOSS 41

CHAPTER FOUR 49
TINA 49
BROWN 49

CHAPTER FIVE 57
CARLENE 57
CORSEY 57

CHAPTER SIX 75
THERESA 75
FORD 75

CHAPTER SEVEN 87
QUEEN G 87
SHONTA GIBSON 87

CHAPTER EIGHT 105
MARIAH 105
JERIDO 105

CHAPTER TEN 115
TERESA 115
KEMP 115

CHAPTER ELEVEN 149
NAKENDRA 149
HARRIS-MASON 149

FACES OF RAP MOTHERS – BOOK TWO

CHAPTER TWELVE 165
    LENA 165
    MOSS 165

CHAPTER THIRTEEN 177
    SUGA T 177

CHAPTER FOURTEEN 195
    DE'MIA 195
    WILKINS-ROSEBAUGH 195

CHAPTER FIFTEEN 203
    BONNIE 203
    WILLIAMS 203

ABOUT THE AUTHOR 211
    CANDY STROTHER 211
    DEVORE MITCHELL 211

SOCIAL MEDIA 213
    AND 213
    WEBSITES 213

MERCHANDISE 223
    AND 223
    GIFTS 223

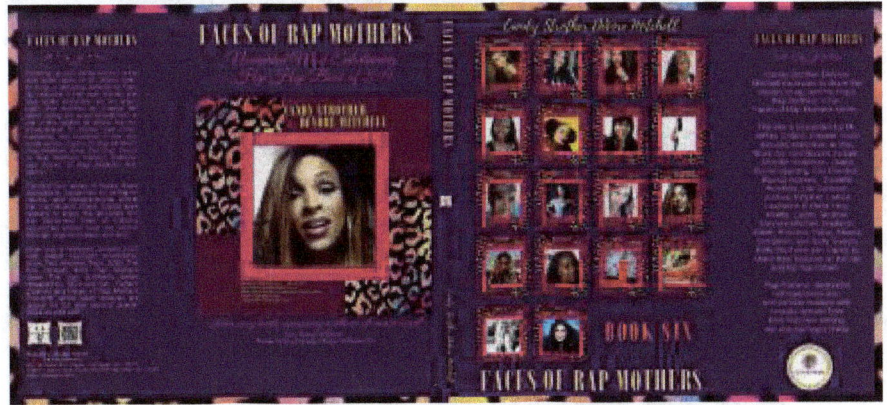

DonnaInk Publications, L.L.C. | Beat Deep Books Copyright Protected

Candy Strother DeVore Mitchell
FACES OF RAP MOTHERS
BOOK THREE

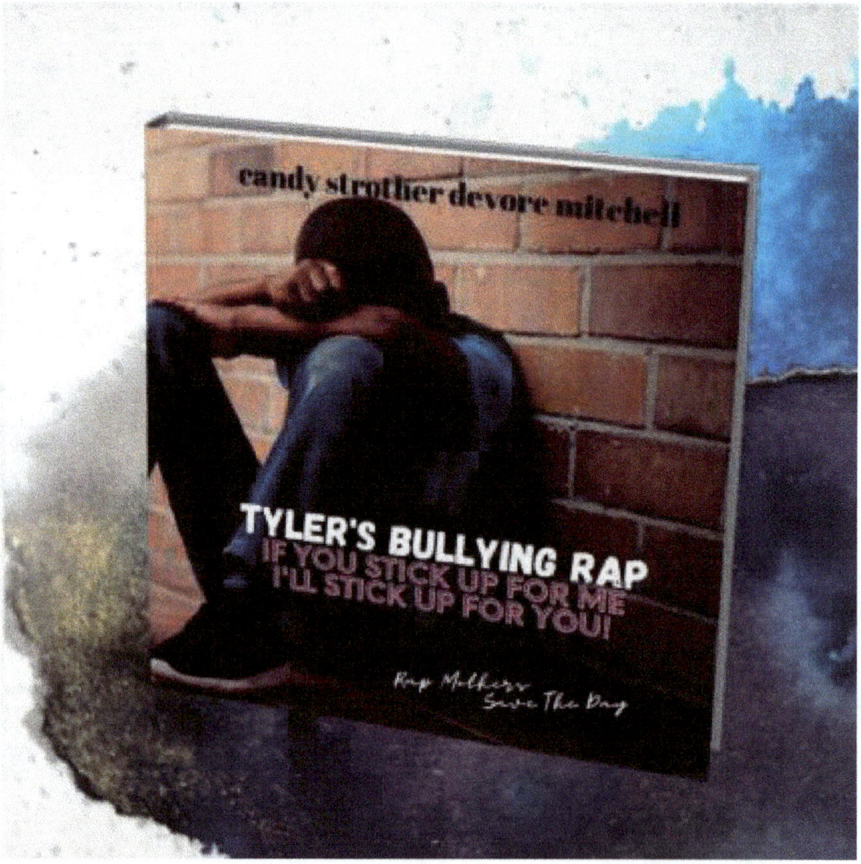
candy strother devore mitchell
TYLER'S BULLYING RAP
IF YOU STICK UP FOR ME
I'LL STICK UP FOR YOU!
Rap Mothers
Save The Day

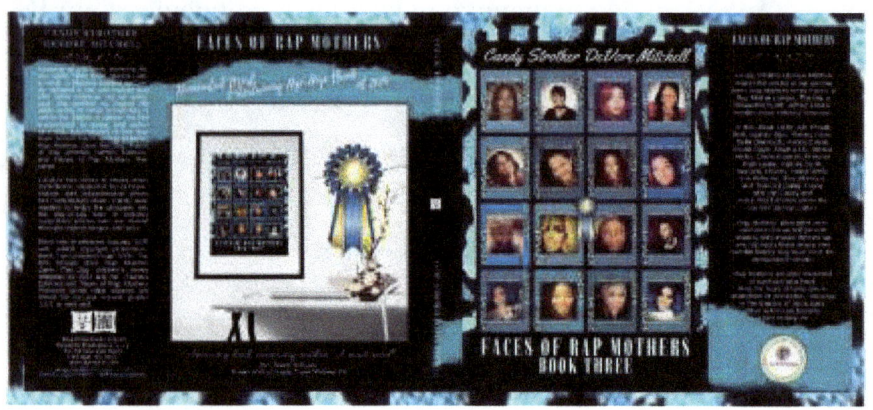

EPIGRAPH

MOSS DEF

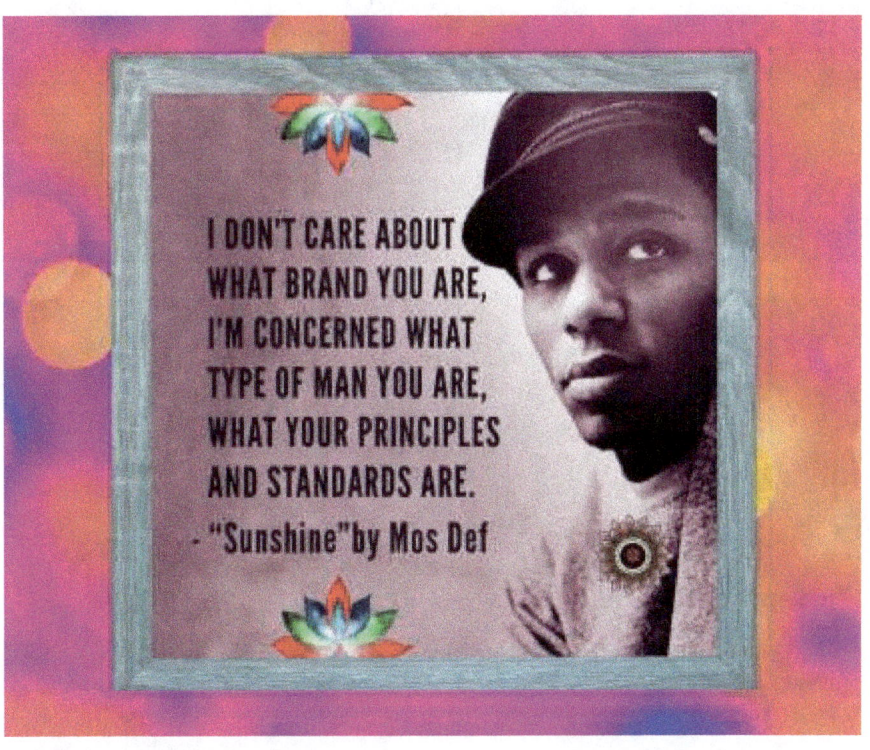

BEING
A
TWIN
Me And My Best Friend
candy strother
devore mitchell

COMBO
HARD COVER COLOR
Books One thru Four
BOOK
FOUR

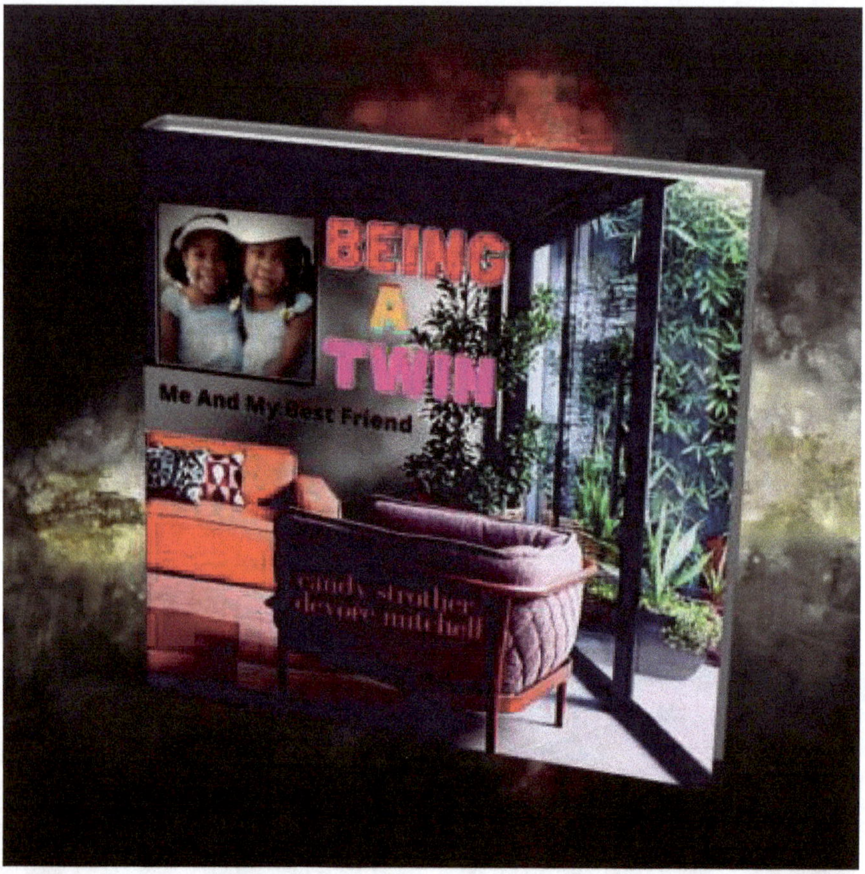

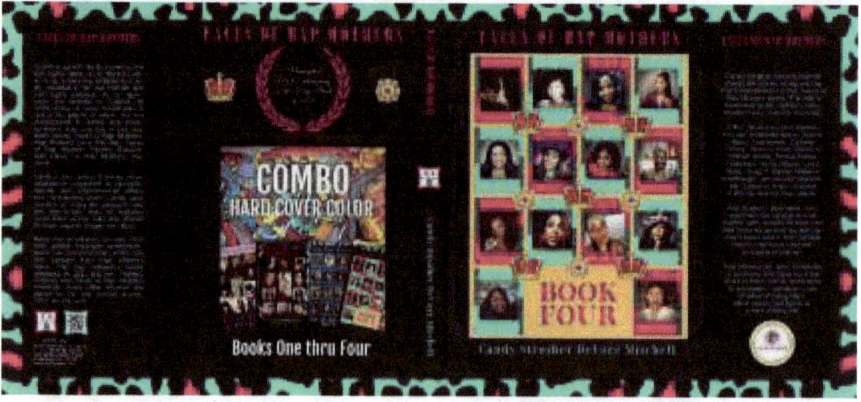

FOREWORD

JEFFREY COLLINS

CANDY STROTHER DEVORE MITCHELL

CANDICE STROTHER DEVORE-MITCHELL AS THE ORIGINAL RAP MOTHER has included civil and human rights advocacy throughout her life following her Aunt Ophelia DeVore. While not as prolific as Aunt Ophelia – it is difficult at the very least for "anyone" to follow in her aunt's shoes – but Candice represents a strong integer in progressive advocacy for the rights and freedoms of all persons.

Additionally, Candice has remained immersed within the entertainment industry since her early youth. With an extended family deeply entrenched in performance arts and advocacies, she has been raised among notable icons and these individuals are mentioned and/or presented throughout impending chapters of this, the fourth title in the "Faces of Rap Mothers" series.

Two of Candice's children, HONEY and KING THA RAPPER, are hip-hop artists. HONEY is in the "Official Group X" group. KING THA RAPPER is working as an independent and has, in the past, been approached by Hollywood Records – a connection being revisited in the current hour. Their activities and Strother's engagement with the industry on theirs and others behalf, resulted in *Faces of Rap Mothers*™ multiple book series (over five at this time), a reality television series on varied networks, corporatization of Faces of Rap Mothers, and two subsidiaries (thus far) 1) a Roku television network and 2) the Faces of Rap Mothers Group.

Included in *Faces of Rap Mothers*™ – *Book Four* are "new" contributory stories, along with some former favorites, with images, biographies, and/or back stories Faces of Rap Mothers™. Readers, rap, and hip-hop fans enjoy.

My sincere congratulation to Candice on her newest book release and all associated business initiatives.

*Donna*Ink Publications, L.L.C. | Beat Deep Books Copyright Protected

About Jeffrey Collins:

Mr. Collins heads *Universal Digital Distribution*. He is a senior business consultant for several major artists and entertainment companies including, Famous Music Group. Having managed agencies, and booking well-known acts such as Dusty Springfield, Joe Cocker, Led Zeppelin, Lonnie Donegan, Moody Blues, The Beatles, etc. artisans Collins represented also included soul singer Donnie Elbert and Warren Davis Monday Band, etc., Jeffrey began a chain of retail record stores and a wholesale distribution company throughout the 70's and into the early 80's. He also produced recording artists, developing Echo Records and Vista Sounds. He created reggae albums with releases from Dennis Brown, Gregory Issacs, Johnny Clarke, etc. with over one hundred (100) additional famous artists. His vocation brought more internationally known artists and producers from Europe, Jamaica, and the United States. In 1983, he set-up an independent recording studio in Englewood, New Jersey and achieved great successes.

From this base, JC successfully worked with Adina Howard, Boogie Down Productions / KRS-ONE, Brenda K. Starr, Chill Rob G., ColonEl Abrams, Father MC, G-DEP, GRAVE-DIGGAZ, Positive K., Ram Squad, Ready for The World, Sunz of Man, Wu-Tang Clan, and a host of other artists that obtained "major label recording deals" with MCA, JIVE, KOCH, and others.

Although he could have retired at 50, when he moved with his family to Coral Springs, Florida, the call of music was still too loud to be ignored. He decided in 2004, to once more enjoy the challenges involved in the recording industry and determined to keep doing what he loves best.

After first setting up a warehouse filled with vinyl records, Jeffrey became a consultant for a record pressing and CD plant, based in Plantation, Florida. He then started a new digital record label, Famous Records, Corporation, which releases and promotes music for artists worldwide via Universal Digital Distribution.

CANDY STROTHER DEVORE MITCHELL

FAMOUS RECORDS / UNIVERSAL DIGITAL

Tel: 954-366-7419 | Cell: 954-817-2878

Skype: jeffrey.echovista | www.UniversalDigitalDistribution.com

Check Out:

Rap Mothers™ Save The Day Children's Series Books!

*Donna*Ink Publications, L.L.C. | *Beat Deep Books Copyright Protected*

ACKNOWLEDGEMENTS
CANDY STROTHER DEVORE MITCHELL

CANDY STROTHER DEVORE MITCHELL

AUTHOR CANDY STROTHER DEVORE-MITCHELL'S vision for *Faces of Rap Mothers* features Gen Y and Z rap and hip-hop Americana with an immersion of history where women share a notable elixir and enchantments in their evolution. This holds true throughout the *Faces of Rap Mothers* vision Mitchell has created, which is growing by leaps and bounds in the current hour. Over one hundred mothers, daughters, sisters, aunts, nieces, cousins, women and, now rap fathers, share stories, histories, and talent as Member movers and shakers. The *Faces of Rap Mothers Enterprise Membership* is being formalized for 2022's onset – another advent moment for Candy Strother DeVore-Mitchell's Enterprise. Along with the rap mothers, are rap fathers, and a suite of new titles *Faces of Rap Mothers Fathers Editions* volumes are also forthcoming with the first volume dropping November of 2021. These works are coupled with *Rap Mothers Save The Day* and *Faces of Rap Mothers Presents* . . . (e.g.: varied groups, entertainers, actors, etc. featured in each volume) and additional guidebooks, new magazines, and additional publications for the Enterprise through DonnaInk Publications, L.L.C. under their Imprints.

The terms: *Faces of Rap Mothers*, *Rap Mothers*, and *Rap Fathers* are under copyright through the publishing house on behalf of Author Candy Strother DeVore-Mitchell who retains rights and trademarks. Alongside these works, official corporate merchandising, magazines, posters, publisher sponsored books, clothing, shoes, carry bags, etc. are continuously in development for entertainment and functional use. As well, many knockoffs are on the Internet, which are "unofficial" and not subject to Unified Purchase Codecs (UPCs), Securities and Exchange Commission (SEC) filings, or Internal Revenue Service (IRS) taxation through the Enterprise as those creations were never approval by the corporation and are third-party creations who answer to the UPC, SEC, and IRS alone. Thus far, legal action has not been taken. These knockoffs are often meant to be complimentary and/or there is a solid misunderstanding regarding merchandising rights, and these are less and less frequent. For "official" merchandising visit

DonnaInk Publications, L.L.C. | Beat Deep Books Copyright Protected

www.facesofrapmothers.com – the "official" website for the *Faces of Rap Mothers Enterprise.*

Capturing early and latent rap and hip-hop tradition under her multiple series books and corporate endeavors has resulted in inclusion of hundreds of entrepreneurial women, men, and children where accolades are shared now throughout the United States and abroad. Candy's first book, "Faces of Rap Mothers Book One" was nominated in the United Kingdom for the following:

"Most Entertaining Hip Hop Book of 2019"

Book Four *Rap Mothers*™:

Faces of Rap Mothers™ *Book Four,* includes many new Rap Mother Members who share intimate stories, biographies, resumes, and more with images listed alphabetically by last name after Candy Strother DeVore-Mitchell:

1. Author Candy Strother DeVore Mitchell
2. Antonette Ames
3. Dianna Boss
4. Tina Brown
5. Carlene Corsey
6. Theresa Ford
7. Queen G (Shonta Gibson)
8. Mariah Jerido
9. Theresa Kemp
10. Nakendra Harris-Mason
11. Lena Moss
12. Suga T

*Donna*Ink Publications, L.L.C. | Beat Deep Books Copyright Protected

13. Demia Wilkens-Rosebaugh
14. Bonnie Williams

Welcome to Faces of Rap Mothers™ – Book Four!

INTRODUCTION

MS. DONNA L. QUESINBERRY

CANDY STROTHER DEVORE MITCHELL

THE FACES OF RAP MOTHERS IS A SMALL, WOman-owned, corporation registered in California that is doing business as, *Faces of Rap Mothers Enterprise*. As such, the *Faces of Rap Mothers Enterprise* is now comprised of two subsidiary business tracks:

1. Faces of Rap Mothers Music Group
2. Faces of Rap Mothers Television Network

Additionally, a new charitable 501 (c)3 is emerging in early 2022; afterward, *Faces of Rap Mothers* stocks are slated to go on sale. However, prior to these ventures, the *Faces of Rap Mothers Enterprise* is beginning "official" memberships and transitioning from media-based membership to an "official" membership organization, which exudes structure and growth. To date, in creation of multi-book(s) series there are the following:

1. *Faces of Rap Mothers Books One through Ten* – this is the original series where Candy Strother DeVore-Mitchell called friends, affiliates, entertainers, family members, etc. and proffered their participation in a book comprised of contributory stories with images.

2. *Rap Mothers Save The Day Books One through Ten* – this is the secondary suite of books where Candy Strother DeVore-Mitchell desired to create children's titles with contributory ghostwriter in her niece. This series includes rap mothers coming to the rescue, with exception of book three that moves to a story about twins, where book four will return to the "save the day" platform.

3. *Faces of Rap Mothers Fathers Editions One through Ten* – this is a spin-off of the rap mothers' books and is the rap father equivalent and includes some seriously high-profile rap fathers . . . first volume is releasing November of 2022 after a COVID related delay in early 2021.

4. *Faces of Rap Mothers Presents . . . Books One through Ten* – this is a solid performer based series where contributors and/or members have rising star status and have been selected for a "presents" book; thus far the Faces of Rap Mothers are presenting Group X – a collection of young adult female rap artists on the teen scene; Curvy Queens of Dallas – a collection of curvy queens who are topping the charts with their songs and national anthem; Bonnie

FACES OF RAP MOTHERS – BOOK TWO

Williams Photojournaling Snapshot – this is a story about Mrs. Bonnie Williams – the late Stanley "Tookie" Williams wife . . .

It has been very unfortunate as publisher to *Faces of Rap Mothers*, the book(s) series' – along with all of the DonnaInk Publications, L.L.C.'s works, were put on hold in spring of 2021 until mid-summer when production was resumed on our books. It was not our intention to delay our titles and impact pre-sale purchasers who are genuinely appreciated; however, the stop was due to circumstances outside the publishing house's control and as a small, woman-owned, publisher providing traditional publication to authors – there are times where Acts of God and circumstances outside of our control happen. However, production is back on cue and happily these newest titles are producing once more.

This, Book Four, of the Faces of Rap Mothers "original" series includes a solid suite of contributors. "Some" contributions are lean and others meatier. While some contributions resemble resumes, there are those stories that are sensitive and personal. The interesting element is each contributor approaches their gift to you as readers in a unique stylus. Some submissions were not received by the original production date / time – typically these are the "leaner" chapters. Candy Strother DeVore-Mitchell wrote more of the contributory chapters for submitters in this book, while images were forwarded to her attention. One or two chapters feature 100% of Candy's effort to compile and draft the content.

As the ghostwriter with credit – I make a strong attempt to keep Candy Strother DeVore-Mitchell's voice while revamping her composition. Candy is the first person to state she is not a writer as much as a storyteller and a conjoiner of stories. She is epic at identifying participants and future members of her platform and for gaining their engagement. Her capability to do so is a "WOW" factor. Not every Diva with a following who has a ghostwriter is comfortable sharing that knowledge with readers and fans or aficionados but Candy does keep it real in this regard. She supports the ideal of getting yours and this is something that really draws people in when she approaches them.

Each contributor to Candy Strother DeVore-Mitchell's book(s) series extend a hand of gratitude for her inclusion of their story and their media in her varied books and now music group and television network. Ms. DeVore-Mitchell is one of a group of few who proffer the ability to join her platform, be published, be enabled to produce expert engineered music, and to share programming on a television network.

So . . . here you have the newest selection of Faces of Rap Mothers Book Four Contributors who have happily provided their compilation toward the collection of series book(s) as part of the Enterprise platform.

A special thank you to all contributors and in turn for them to Candy Strother DeVore-Mitchell who provides a continuum of new opportunities for members' benefit.

Look for Faces of Rap Mothers Presents . . . Group X second week of November 2021, Faces of Rap Mothers Fathers Editions Book One week of Thanksgiving 2021, Faces of Rap Mothers Book Five last week of November 2021, and Faces of Rap Mothers Book Six the second week of December 2021. Additionally, two children's books, "Tyler's Bullying Rap" and "Being a Twin" are releasing between this title and the holiday season. There are also surprise releases coming soon!

These titles are meant for entertainment purposes and while within, here and there, are some true historical nuggets – the reality is – this is docufiction or autobiographical fiction. As publisher, and ghostwriter with credit, every effort is completed to validate statements of fact through research and there are areas where research just is not available; however, each story is traced to associations and the reasonable ability for what is stated to be true in regarding to being affiliated in the information shared and that being accurate. Where "media" through journalism and/or records tracing – birth, death, marriage, etc. – may conflict with stories – the takeaway is left to the reader as over term, thus far, the truth appears at times to be what is presented by contributors, other times questionable, and then landing typically somewhere in the middle.

Stories and storytelling are arts where interpretation is often resting with the perspective of a person's experience. Being that everyone's experience is their own and through a different lens of viewpoint – there are many times a truth can be many things to many people. We do not represent the veracity of stories herein, but we do validate the basics of person, place, thing, etc. are accurate. Enjoy this, Book Four, and look for Book Five later this month!

FACES OF
RAP MOTHERS

CHAPTER ONE

CANDY STROTHER DEVORE MITCHELL

CANDY STROTHER DEVORE MITCHELL

HEY Y'ALL WE ARE BACK AGAIN! *Faces of Rap Mothers* is an ongoing true reality entertainment platform featuring Hollywood happenings and events that keep popping. Since book three, *Faces of Rap Mothers Enterprise* has purchased a television network (*Faces of Rap Mothers Television Network*) and created the *Faces of Rap Mothers Group* (A select group of rap mothers creating music together that sounds smoove!). Both our television network, and music group, are new business verticals under the Enterprise. The good news is, we are growing!

Jeffrey McDaniel's *Verb'z Up Magazine*, Mark Rowe's *Soul Central* – UK, Queen G's *Let's Got To Work Entertainment* and *Untouchable Magazine* – US have continued showing Faces of Rap Mothers Members love through stories and honorable mentions.

Earlier this year, we streamed live and online through MJOwn-Network, Muuzictyme, Now Network, and Smile Network, which are aired using Amazon Firestick, Apple TV, MJOwnNetwork App (e.g.: Internet WiFi) and, of course, on ROKU. Summer of 2021, after purchasing our network, *Faces of Rap Mothers* left some of these former networks; however, sincere gratitude for services previously provided remains close to our heart.

Faces of Rap Mothers has also continued to be promoted through *High Desert 100.9 The Heat* by DJ Craig EC – a local SoCal / Phoenix icon; *Los Angeles Power 106 Big Boy In The Mornings*; and *Louisiana CJM Music Management FM Radio Show*.

The passage of time since *Faces of Rap Mothers Book Three* has featured difficulties in the loss of three close friends and relatives, such as *King of Stage Bobby Brown Jr.* who is a very close friend of my family; also, my eldest son's grandfather, *Big Ricardo Senior* passed; and, of course, year one of the platform, our beloved *Rap Mother Jamie Paris* suddenly passed. The entire *Faces of Rap Mothers* entourage were heartbroken in devastating shock over these losses; especially saddened about Jamie Paris as she was near and dear to us all. Angel Hicks (OG Lil Mama), HONEY BLUNT (West Coast Hip Hop Artist), and Sharon Lynette Young (Beretta) paid respects to Queen Jamie in celebration of her amazing life. Personally, I knew Jamie from age fourteen onward; she was JP Cali Smoov's (Hip Hop Star) mother and remains the continuous Queen Angel to *Faces of Rap Mothers*. I pray they all rest in peace and include Artist Nipsey Hustle and the world-famous Kobe Bryant of Laker Nation.

As far as KING THA RAPPER, he has been keeping busy writing and producing with *Black Cash Universal Studios* as an entertainment artist. KING is producing the up, and coming, album featuring my nephew LKapone's (e.g.: Gary Indiana and Midwest Artist). They have created some beautiful music and hot tracks!

My daughter HONEY has also been writing and recording daily. She began engineering music training. I must admit, she is surprisingly good at it and learns fast. HONEY began a musical group with her peers ... the ... *Official Group X*. They have been performing at *Comedy Cochella's* and additional high-end events and are soon releasing an album. They sound beautiful together. A new book, through DonnaInk Publications, L.L.C. and their Beat Deep Books Imprint, features Group X, "Faces of Rap Mothers Presents ... Group X" ya'll need to check it out.

My son Lawrence completed United States Army service and returned home. It is a blessing having him at home once again – I mentioned this previously in volume three I believe, but it is worth a second mention.

I went to the soccer field and spent time with my son, and athlete, Tyler Lee - he and his soccer team (e.g.: AV AZTECS) continue training for championship seasons. While there, I gave him a copy of the latest *Faces of Rap Mother* book, which gave him a big smile in front of his coach and team players. This was one of the happiest moments in my life – just seeing his smile.

I keep my children and friends in my daily prayers because God's power is the best and as a Mother I rely on His Word.

Through *Faces of Rap Mothers*, there are continual talents that excite me . . . Roxie is one of them, she is a super model with a strong history of professional modeling, and she is also a vocalist. She has the lungs of a Whitney Houston, and I am truly looking forward to watching her career grow. She is incredible.

On the human rights front, Gilbert, APA Affiliates People's Alliance (APA) Creator along with Stanley "Tookie" William's wife, also a famous human rights activist, Bonnie Williams, and her son Trayvon Williams, and I continue the fight for *human and children rights of all humanity*. Keep an eye out on *Faces of Rap Mothers Television Network* for exciting and entertaining stories from *Faces of Rap Mothers Enterprise* and our channel programmers, which are intended to include human rights initiatives alongside other entertainment channel productions.

As I look back on the first half of 2021, and 2020, life has been a roller-coaster largely due to the pandemic and COVID, which continues to plague us. However, my time has been fruitful as my book series continue to thrive with *Faces of Rap Mothers* volumes five and six releasing prior to Holiday Season 2021; *Rap Mothers Save The Day* series volumes three and four also releasing prior to Holiday Season 2021; first volume of *Faces of Rap Mothers Fathers Editions* releasing November 2021 in time for Thanksgiving; and *Faces of Rap*

Mothers Presents . . . *Group X* releasing early November 2021. Thankfully, I have the advantage of a good publisher with an exceptionally talented ghostwriter or associate writer who has become a rap mother and is a part of my corporate leadership.

With my initial *Faces of Rap Mothers* volume nominated by *Soul Central Magazine's* Chief Executive Officer (CEO) as "Most Entertaining Hip Hop Book of 2019" – I remain enormously proud and humbled – my books are beautiful – I love them personally and I am thankful others do as well.

Last input for this volume, is that all my rap mothers feature incredible stories – it is my hope you enjoy *Faces of Rap Mothers* and appreciate the reality as this ten-volume book series expands – an additional ten-volumes are forthcoming because our rap mothers, and now, rap fathers continue to increase in number, and each has a story to contribute. As I continue to pinch myself – again - we are at over one hundred members and counting! So, keep reading with us.

It is my sincere hope as readers and believers eventually this full collection, which will feature combination discounts through my publisher, will soon be embraces as true collector's editions while our television and music platforms grow and expand.

Be blessed in the remainder of 2021 and into the New Year of 2022!

CANDY STROTHER DEVORE MITCHELL

CANDY STROTHER DEVORE MITCHELL

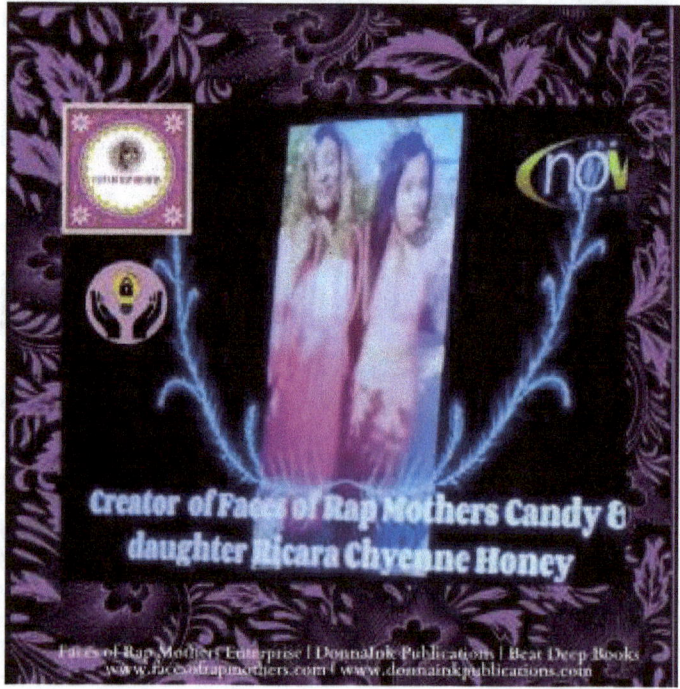

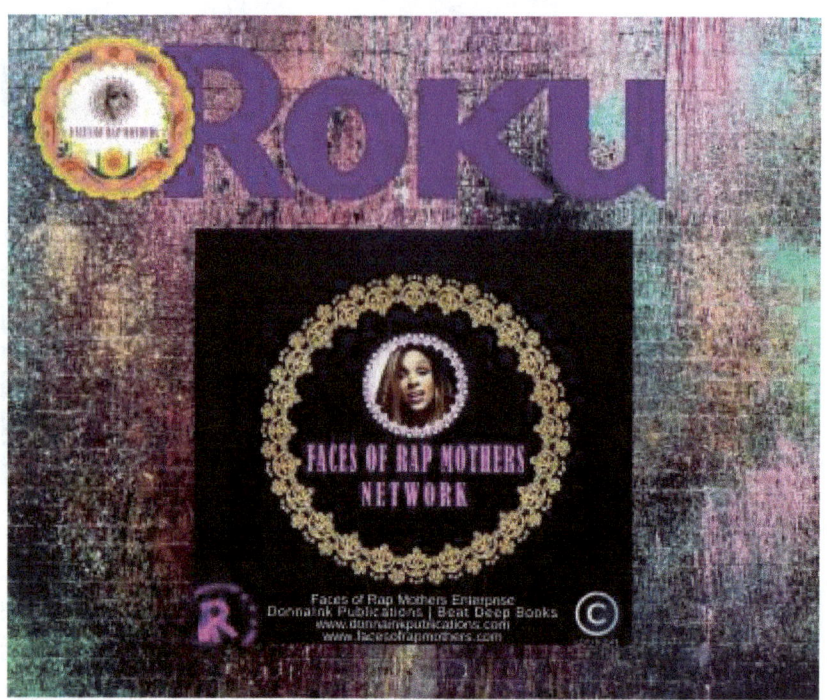

FACES OF RAP MOTHERS – BOOK FOUR

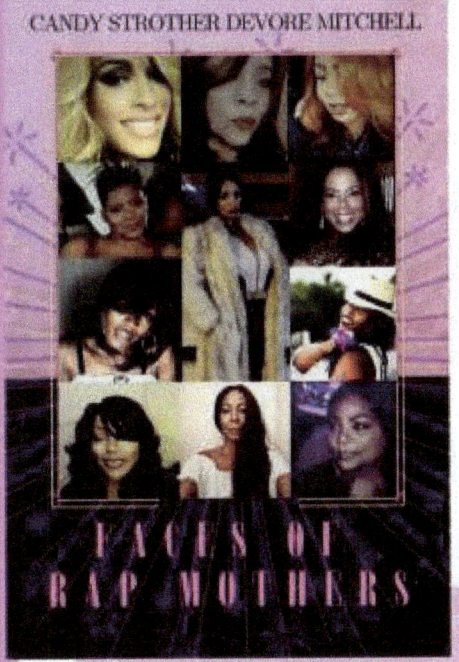

DonnaInk Publications through Beat Deep Books

Press Kit

PG. 2
Faces of Rap Mothers Short Review

PG. 3
Candy Strother DeVore Mitchell Bio

PG. 4 - 5
Sample Questions & Answers

PG. 7
Press Release

PG. 8 - 9
Fact and Sell Sheets

PG. 10
Information Sheet

"A solid visual expose of the stories behind the scenes of rap and hip-hop's icons."

DonnaInk Publications, L.L.C. | Beat Deep Books Copyright Protected

CANDY STROTHER DEVORE MITCHELL

FACES OF RAP MOTHERS REVIEW

"Faces of Rap Mothers," by Candy Strother DeVore Mitchell is an expose of the families surrounding rap and hip-hop industry icons.

What makes a family great? This is a question philosophers have shared generation to generation. Just where is the defining line between family and successful futures? While "Faces of Rap Mothers," does not intend to reeducate the myopia of com-plexities inflicted upon the rap and hip-hop trans-cendence, it does involve a collective congru-ence toward redefined futures of what have sometimes been distressed histories. It resonates within a modern landscape where right, and wrong in America's epic is demonstrated as bling and zing and as talismans of success.

Candy's minimalist conceptualism of life among Hollywood's rap and hip-hop stars, shares poignant snapshots among familial confines without glamour complicating life. Even though the result is initiative-taking outcomes, which resolutely elevated entire familial lineage – that is not the intent here. "Faces of Rap Mothers," is an intriguing capsule of rap and hip-hop derived from a familial perspec-tive. It is eye-opening and authentic. Poignant and authoritative. A solid visual expose of the stor-ies behind the scenes of rap and hip-hop icons.

"The power of Faces of Rap Mothers is the collective drive toward redefined futures"

FACES OF RAP MOTHERS REVIEW

"Faces of Rap Mothers," by Candy Strother DeVore Mitchell is an expose of the families surrounding rap and hip-hop industry icons.

What makes a family great? This is a question philosophers have shared generation to generation. Just where is the defining line between family and successful futures? While "Faces of Rap Mothers," does not' intend to reeducate the myopia of complexities inflicted upon the rap and hip-hop transcendence, it does involve a collective congruence toward redefined futures of what have sometimes been distressed histories. It resonates within a modern landscape where right, and wrong, in America's epic represent bling and zing as talismans for success.

Candy's minimalist conceptualism of life among Hollywood's rap and hip-hop stars, shares poignant snapshots among familial confines without the glamour that complicates life even though it resulted in initiative-taking outcomes that resolutely elevated entire family's lineage.

"Faces of Rap Mothers," is an intriguing capsule of rap and hip-hop derived from a familial perspective. It is eye-opening and authentic. Poignant and authoritative. A solid visual expose of the stories behind the scenes of rap and hip-hop icons.

"The power of Faces of Rap Mothers is the collective drive toward redefined futures"

4

CANDY STROTHER DEVORE MITCHELL

Candy Strother DeVore Mitchell is the niece of a civil rights leader who worked directly alongside Dr. Martin Luther King. This may have resulted in her burgeoning interests as a human rights activist. Ms. Mitchell has testified on Capitol Hill and aired in national news broadcasts regarding newsworthy topics. She is the creator and executive producer of The Face of Rap Mothers, an affiliation of women leaders in the rap industry who work in unison to build better futures for humanity through entrepreneurial, solopreneur and philanthropic efforts. Candy is the Owner and Chairwoman of her woman-owned small business Faces of Rap Mothers Enterprise, which includes Faces of Rap Mothers Music Group and Faces of Rap Mothers Television Network. Candy is also CEO of Black Cash Universal Studios Entertainment.

EXCERPT

Within the rap and hip-hop mindset, driving beats and hard-hitting lyrical spits – result in greater awareness of the human condition. Women contributors to this, the first edition and volume of the *Faces of Rap Mothers Series*, remain acutely aware of the stature of their universe regarding fans and aficionados who reflect on, and often mirror, lifestyles of rap and hip-hop icons. Disclosure regarding facts families associated with rap and hip-hop reflect, include upwardly mobile and surprisingly routine American Dream realizations, mitigated within the backdrop of the music. Readers as fans and aficionados may benefit in learning more about these truths. Faces of Rap Mother authors' children attend gifted and talented programs, participate in music studies, take acting classes, and work diligently to be successful understanding their roots and all it has taken to rise above history while embracing quality futures.

Beyond origins of rap and hip-hop, linear patterns of music production and its development, infused with rap and hip-hop from cultural inclusions of the Caribbean and West Africa. Of course, South American, Middle Eastern, and Indian influences resonant rap and hip-hop performance art – expressly in the current hour. There are elements of European folk music now and again heard in backdrops and riffs but the pulse of modern rap and hip-hop is solely American. It formed in, and around, American urban / inner-city experiences where street performers and underground movements hold solid resonance.

Faces of Rap Mothers takes readers behind the scenes providing often "little known" or "virtually unknown" morsels - fun facts of interest - and unwitting asides. Knowing there is more than meets the eye, no matter the artform or genre, is always exciting; and, more importantly, Faces of Rap Mothers entertains readers, fans, and aficionados hence the creation of our stories.

This is the first volume of the *Faces of Rap Mothers Series*. Each volume will feature unique contributors and their backstories and/or elaborate of prior contributors' stories as well.

By Christmas 2021, Faces of Rap Mothers Books One through Six, Faces of Rap Mothers Fathers Editions Book One, Faces of Rap Mothers Presents Group X, and additional Rap Mothers Save the Day children's stories, which feature "save the day" events except book three that shares the story of twins.

FACES OF RAP MOTHERS – BOOK FOUR

"Faces of Rap Mothers shares stories of human triumph from potentially adverse origins"

SAMPLE QUESTIONS

1. What motivated you to write, "FACES OF RAP MOTHERS?"
2. Where did the story idea come from?
3. Is this your first book?
4. What drove you to write this title?
5. Can you share what you feel readers will derive from FACES OF RAP MOTHERS?
6. Are you intending to perform book signings?
7. Are you attending any festivals or book fairs?
8. Have you drafting a new book?
9. Have you thought about a screenplay for the title?
10. What writing prompts or writing practices aided you in creating this title?

> "Moving from oneself to thine own self can be a dance among the stars of the night skies."

SAMPLE ANSWERS

1. The motivation behind FACES OF RAP MOTHERS remains life and how to work through it.
2. The story idea for FACES OF RAP MOTHERS is from the life experiences of participants.
3. FACES OF RAP MOTHERS is my first nonfiction novel.
4. Well, this is like question two (2) but to elaborate – what drove this title is the life events I encountered where I grew up under the umbrella of rap and hip hop and then raised my family under that same umbrella.
5. I believe readers can benefit from FACES OF RAP MOTHERS for the resonance is shares.
6. I schedule book signings through my publisher.
7. My publisher, **DonnaInk Publications, L.L.C.** – my title is under their **Beat Deep Books** Imprint – will be identifying book events to attend and I intend to attend events within my immediate area and expand from there.
8. I now have over one hundred rap mothers and, rap fathers – a new addition; however, I am incredibly happy to be fortunate in doing so.
9. FACES OF RAP MOTHERS would do well in screenplay I believe, and I would consider it.
10. Writing practices, I can identify for readers desiring to write is to take your idea and put it on paper. Of 200M people wanting to author a book – only 100K do.

FACES OF RAP MOTHERS – BOOK FOUR

PRESS RELEASE

Faces of Rap Mothers by Candy Strother DeVore Mitchell available in pre-release

"Faces of Rap Mothers," by Candy Strother DeVore Mitchell is a first of its kind collaborative compilation, published by Beat Deep Books. *Source:* [Beat Deep Books](#)

CARTHAGE, N.C. - June 7, 2019 - PRLog -- "Faces of Rap Mothers," by Candy Strother DeVore Mitchell is a first of its kind collaborative compilation, published by Beat Deep Books. This title shares gallery images and back-stories of women who are artists, business owners, relatives or mothers of Rap and Hip-Hop's most infamous Superstar Icons. Candy's minimalist approach, represents the important women who educated, nursed, represented, supported, and upheld Rap and Hip-Hop through their shadowing of its Icons or self-exposure as artisans within the industry. These women rise, oftentimes in the shadows of Ultra-Famous Rap and Hip-Hop performers, who they love. One can only imagine being a cousin, niece, mother, sister, or wife of an infamous personality. Quietly observing the rank and file within media, and the music industry, experiencing the waves of success involve with their ebbs and flows in the tides of life, the extreme highs and extreme lows of the path of stardom must inure even the strongest of these women; however, elements of soul remain at the core of their lives and it is demonstrated in, "Faces of Rap Mothers." Contributors to Ms. Mitchell's book include:

Beretta (e.g.: Sharon Lynette Young), CEO of one of the hottest recording studios in Hollywood where some rap and hip-hop superstars record. Her chapter is certain to entice future music entrepreneurs interested in engineering soulful sounds.

Honey Blunt, a six (6) time award-winning West Coast recording artist; is also a model and dancer as a well-known Rap and Hip-Hop entertainer. Her sultry personality shines in revelations of the boundaries of emergent music trends she fashions to a taste of honey in golden performances.

Monica Davis, ex-wife of a well-known R&B star (we will learn who in her excerpt), grew up in Hollywood after spending years touring with Ralph Tresvant Sr. (e.g.: also known as Rizz and Rizzo, American actor, record producer, singer, and songwriter best known as New Edition's Lead Singer). She also dated very influential rap and hip-hop artists who include LL COOL J, Jessie D., and Johnny Gill, Jr.

Angel Gilcrest-Guyton – illustrious rap and hip-hop celebrity formerly married to two (2) Superstar Producers and an independent woman in her own right – more to come . . .

Queen G (e.g.: Shonta Gibson), award-winning CEO and Owner of Letsgotowork Entertainment Network; also, Animateur de radio at BlackOut Radio and Media Director at CLUB HIS HOP Las Vegas, grew up in Hollywood where she performed as a movie extra. Queen G is Superstar Tyrese's sister.

Tyaunna Harris, actor and model, grew up within Rap and Hip-Hop and keeps her finger on speed-dial within the industry today . . . we will learn more about Tyaunna very soon . . .

O.G. LIL MAMA (e.g.: Angel Hicks), West Coast Hip-Hop Artist grew up with Snoop Dogg. What else is there to say? Looking forward to this slice of music industry history . . .

Lena Moss, Superstar Aaron Hall's wife and mother of beautiful Kaloni Hall, Lena and Aaron's daughter. Aaron Hall is an American singer and songwriter whose debut album sold over a million copies and is certified platinum.

Jamie Paris, mother of one of Snoop Dogg's recording artist, JP Cali Smoov discloses the facts about living the life of a Rap and Hip-Hop Mother.

Nina Womack, award-winning actor, event producer and filmmaker is also the Founder of Transmedia 360" a multimedia and branding agency. Nina has an extensive background in event production, festival, film, and theater. She is also the creator of "Let's Be Whole" (e.g.: an interactive, grassroots outreach program designed to reach communities of color at elevated risk for cancer, disease, mental illness, obesity, poverty, and other stress-related trauma.). Her son is a producer, and she is the niece of Superstar Bobby Womack.

About the Author: Candy Strother DeVore Mitchell is the niece of a civil rights leader who worked directly alongside Dr. Martin Luther King. This may have resulted in her burgeoning interests as a human rights activist. Candy has testified on Capitol Hill and aired in national news broadcasts regarding newsworthy topics. She is the creator and executive producer of "The Face of Rap Mothers," an affiliation of women leaders in the rap industry who work in unison to build better futures for humanity through entrepreneurial, solopreneur and philanthropic efforts. Candy is also the CEO of Black Cash Universal Studios Entertainment, and her son is King Tha Rapper – she shares her story in an introductory chapter of, "Faces of Rap Mothers."

To contact the author, write to: contact@donnainkpublications.com or facesofrapmothers@gmail.com

FACT SHEET

Title:	Faces of Rap Mothers.
Author:	Ms. Candy Strother DeVore Mitchell
Publisher:	DonnaInk Publications, L.L.C. | Beat Deep Books Imprint
	601 McReynolds Street, Carthage, NC 28327
Publication Date:	1 October 2019; Due to an unauthorized copy – re-released February of 2020.
Product Details:	Library of Congress Cataloging-in-Publication
	Mitchell, Candy Strother DeVore
	Quesinberry, Donna – ghostwriter w/credit
	Faces of Rap Mothers
	199 p. cm.
	Identifiers: ISBN – 13 – 978-1-947704-32-9 (alk. color paper); 13: 978-1-947704-30-5 (alk. b/w paper); 13: 978-1-947704-31-2 (alk. color hardback w/dust cover); 13: 978-1-947704-16-9 (alk. b/w hardback w/dust cover) | ISBN – 978-1-947704-24-4 (digital).
First Edition:	10 9 8 7 6 5 4 3 2 1
BIASC:	BIO004000-BIOGRAPHY & AUTOBIOGRAPHY/Music;
	BIO032000 -BIOGRAPHY & AUTOBIOGRAPHY / Social Activists
Cover Art:	dpInk Ltd. Liability Company – Ms. Donna L. Quesinberry
Price:	Soft Cover US $35.00 color
	Hardcover US $45.00 color

2021 DISTRIBUTION AND MARKETING

Wholesalers & Distributors	Amazon Advantage, Atlas Distribution, Baker & Taylor, BCH, Bookmasters, Bulk Books, Cardinal Publishers Group, Consortium, Hummingbird, IngramSpark, IPG, ITASCA Books, ListenUp Indie Pub, Midpoint, National Book Network, New Leaf, Publisher's Group West, SCB Distributors, Small Press United, Smashwords.

DONNAINK PUBLICATIONS, L.L.C. AFFILIATIONS

ABA	AMAZON UK	AMAZON USA	Barnes & Noble	Book Depository	Books-a-Million
Draft2Digital	Espresso Books	IBPA	Ingram	KDP	Lightning Source
PubEasy	NookPress	SPAN			

2021 MARKETING PLAN

Expand on social media fan base build authors have generated. Move blogs to blog trends - gain over 100K followers – work toward 1M. Generate reader group and online media interest building out the authors' organic fan base. Use author blogs as introductions generating interest in the story, the story behind the story and the life of the author. Expand back-links building out social influence marketing to reach over 5M potential readers. Press releases. Press kit. Request review from recognized distributor resources. Demonstrate traffic aggregates of author's social media to gain prospective broadcast programming. Expand reviews and generate humble sensationalism. Radio broadcasts. News publications reviews. Speaking engagements (contingent upon author capability). Develop working list of awards (three [3] publisher covers cost) - "others" for author to fund. Identify additional "free" award resources. Send reader copies to target and secondary markets. Identify in press and news media the impending trajectory about the title. Generate list of additional reviewers and/or buyers. Identify distributors who demonstrate interest based on social media influence, readership reviews, and sales to market and promote for DonnaInk Publications, L.L.C. in representation of this and "other" titles to generate more significant sales. Participate in book conventions and "other" events that will benefit bringing this original novel into the hands of readers.

FACES OF RAP MOTHERS – BOOK FOUR

SELL SHEET

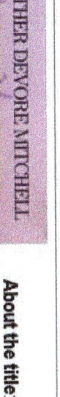

CANDY STROTHER DEVORE MITCHELL

FACES OF RAP MOTHERS

Author Candy Strother DeVore Mitchell

About the title:

Faces of Rap Mothers, by Candy Strother DeVore Mitchell is a first of its kind collaborative compilation, published by **DonnaInk** Publications, L.L.C. through their Beat Deep Books Imprint. This title shares gallery images and back-stories of women who are artists, business owners, relatives or mothers of rap and hip-hop's most Superstar Icons. Candy's minimalist approach, represents the important women who educated, nursed, represented, supported, and upheld rap and hip-hop through their shadowing of its icons or self-exposure as artisans within the industry. These women rise oftentimes in the shadow of ultra-famous rap and hip-hop performers who they love. One can only imagine being a cousin, niece, mother, sister, or wife of an infamous personality. Quietly observing the rank and file within media, the music industry, experiencing the waves of success involve with their ebbs and flows in the tides of life, the extreme highs, and extreme lows of the path of stardom, must inure even the strongest of these women; however, elements of soul remain at the core of their lives, and it is demonstrated in, Faces of Rap Mothers. This is also a first in now "five" series of books centered on the Faces of Rap Mothers Enterprise (a California corporation) platform with hundreds of members.

Author Bio:

Candy Strother DeVore Mitchell is the niece of a civil rights leader who worked directly alongside Dr. Martin Luther King. This may have resulted in her burgeoning interests as a human rights activist. Ms. Mitchell has testified on Capitol Hill and aired in national news broadcasts regarding newsworthy topics. She is the creator and executive producer of The Face of Rap Mothers, an affiliation of women leaders in the rap industry who work in unison to build better futures for humanity through entrepreneurial, solopreneur and philanthropic efforts. Candy is the Owner and Chairwoman of her woman-owned small business Faces of Rap Mothers Enterprise, which includes Faces of Rap Mothers Music Group and Faces of Rap Mothers Television Network. Candy is also CEO of Black Cash Universal Studios Entertainment.

Account:	Account Number:	Quantity	Date:
PO:	Shipper:	Air | Sea | Land:	

DonnaInk Publications, L.L.C., 601 McReynolds Street, Carthage, NC 28327

Website: https://www.donnaink.com **Email:** contact@donnainkpublications.com
Office: (910) 947-3189

Faces of Rap Mothers by Candy Strother DeVore Mitchell	Trim Size Print	6 x 9
	Trim Size Digital	6 x 9
	Page Ct. Print	150
	Page Ct. Digital	Approx. 150
	ISBN Print	
	ISBN Digital	
	Genre	MUS031000-MUSIC / Genres & Styles / Rap & Hip Hop
Suggested Retail: Print: $35.00 Digital: $NVS		

DonnaInk Publications, L.L.C. | Beat Deep Books Copyright Protected

CANDY STROTHER DEVORE MITCHELL

INFORMATION SHEET

Faces of Rap Mothers, by Candy Strother DeVore Mitchell is a first of its kind collaborative compilation, published by Beat Deep Books. This title shares gallery images and back-stories of women who are artists, business owners, relatives or mothers of Rap and Hip-Hop s most infamous Superstar Icons. Candy s minimalist approach, represents the important women who educated, nursed, represented, supported and upheld Rap and Hip-Hop through their shadowing of its Icons or self-exposure as artisans within the industry. These women rise oftentimes in the shadow of Ultra-Famous Rap and Hip-Hop performers who they love. One can only imagine being a cousin, niece, mother, sister or wife of an infamous personality. Quietly observing the rank and file within media, and the music industry, experiencing the waves of success involve with their ebbs and flows in the tides of life, the extreme highs and extreme lows of the path of stardom, must inure even the strongest of these women; however, elements of soul remain at the core of their lives and it is demonstrated in, Faces of Rap Mothers. There are two initial editions, 1) print soft cover and 2) print soft cover as a signature edition with the author and fellow Rap Mother signatures. Releasing in summer of 2019 . . . pre-release purchases are fulfilled "first."

About the Publisher:
DonnaInk Publications, L.L.C. through their **Beat Deep Books Imprint** is representing Mrs. Candy Strother DeVore Mitchell in the publishing and production of, Faces of Rap Mothers.

About the Author:
Candy Strother DeVore Mitchell is the niece of a civil rights leader who worked directly alongside Dr. Martin Luther King. This may have resulted in her burgeoning interests as a human rights activist. Candy has testified on Capitol Hill and aired in national news broadcasts regarding newsworthy topics. She is the creator and executive producer of The Face of Rap Mothers, an affiliation of women leaders in the rap industry who work in unison to build better futures for humanity through entrepreneurial, solopreneur and philanthropic efforts. Candy is also the CEO of Black Cash Universal Studios Entertainment and her son is King Tha Rapper she shares her story in an introductory chapter of, Faces of Rap Mothers.

Bookings:
Candy is available for radio, news and onsite bookings in representation of, Faces of Rap Mothers. She is available for events where an author will befit an event relative within the book and entertainment industry.

Orders:
The most cost-effective manner to purchase, "Faces of Rap Mothers" is through publisher website, visit: https://www.donnaink.com, today.

Bulk Orders:
For bulk orders at significantly higher discounts, write: contact@donnainkpublications.com for more information. **DonnaInk Publications, L.L.C.** adheres to industry standard rate structures for large volume purchases. You can mail a completed Sell Sheet as well.

Interviews:
Candy Strother DeVore Mitchell is available as a public speaker co-authors and participates in interviews. To schedule with him, email candisbook@mail.com.

DonnaInk Publications, L.L.C. | Beat Deep Books Copyright Protected

FACES OF RAP MOTHERS – BOOK FOUR

*Donna*Ink Publications, L.L.C. | *Beat Deep Books Copyright Protected*

CHAPTER TWO

ANTONETTE AMES

About Antonette Ames, Founder & CEO of A H P

As Founder and Chief Executive Officer (CEO) of *Ames High Productions* (A H P), Antonette Ames is the niece of the legendary, late, Sylvester Ames, Jr., President of *A&S Productions*. Sylvester, Antoinette's father, worked with Reverend Marvin Yancy, ex-husband of Natalie Cole (i.e.: daughter of the late Nat King Cole). Sylvester, Marvin, and Kevin Yancy formed *MKS Productions*. Sylvester produced several projects and albums – one of his contributions to industry is *Fountain of Life Joy Choir* with one of the songs lead by Natalie Cole and nominated for a Stellar Award in 1984-85.

Antoinette's mother sang with the gospel group, *The Bernard Sisters*. They sang across Chicago with legendary R&B group, *The Emotions*, known in their early years as, *The Hutchinson Sunbeams*. She also worked with major entertainment artists including, *Rappin 4Tay*, *Mystical*, *Project Pat*, *Evan Lionel*, and *Gerald Kelly*.

It was inevitable Antonette would follow in the footsteps of these great men and women who preceded her within the music industry. Antonette began taking the music industry more seriously in 2004, where she planned church events. She later planned her own major professional events in 2012 and beyond. Starting with a non-profanity gospel comedy show starring comedian Lester Barrie (i.e.: *Def Comedy Jam* all-star, *Apollo Theater* legend, and *BET Comicview Host*); Antonette managed two shows with Lester, an old grammar school classmate of hers from Chicago Illinois. She later held an event with Grammy Award winner *Le'Andria Johnson* in 2015.

Today, Antonette continues in the industry through A H P and shares in *Faces of Rap Mothers Enterprise* reality programming, books, magazines, and additional ventures.

DA Smart

DA Smart was raised in both the Altgeld Murray and Robert Taylor projects. He is now a Chief Executive Officer (CEO), and living legend in Chicago-land area, ready to expand and his feats are well-documented within Chicago.

When DA dropped the Chicago Anthem, *Walk Wit Me* the song was quickly acclaimed as one of the greatest songs ever made in

Chicago hip-hop history. DA Smart has been blessed with the ability to move crowds with his magnetic personality, dynamic energetic stage presence, and entertaining, fun loving, hip-hop talent that spans over two decades. A leader and positive influence within his community, DA Smart has a passion to represent those who are "lost, hungry, naked, and outdoors."

DA's additional amazing talents as a battle and freestyle rapper, have led him to negotiations with big conglomerates such as *Columbia Records, Jive Records, Motown Records,* and *Warner Bros. Records*. He signed to *RCA Records* and later to *Creators Way Associated Labels*, which carried *Twista* and *Do Or Die*. DA holds many milestones that enhanced his career and sold over 10,000 copies in one day at the *Million Man March* in 1995 with his single *One In A Million*.

DA Smart also performed in the video, *Where Ya At*, with *Chuck D, Ice Cube, IceT, Killah Priest,* and *Rza*. He even graced the great Eddie Kendricks video *Get it While It's Hot*. Little known is his prestigious appearances with a star-studded lineup that includes *KRS-One, Poor Righteous Teachers, Prince Markie Dee, A Lighter Shade of Brown, Cypress Hill, Public Enemy,* and *Twista*. He toured Illinois prisons with Mc Lyte and was the first rapper to win the *Regal Talent Show* competition which jettisoned his already burgeoning career.

Now an independent artist, DA is CEO of the talented *Terror Records* label. His branding is continuing the household name built for himself and enhanced through the assistance of team of talents. DA Smart is part of the *Legends of Hip-Hop*, an organization acknowledging contributions of Illinois' Hip-Hop history movers and shakers.

Getting to the Core of the Female Rap Game: *The Qor*

The rap game is challenging. The industry is huge, there are many artists, producers, managers, and record labels to choose from. Some just care about lyrics while others care about beat. There are artists in it for the money and fame, while others are in it to reach those who are lost. The rat race to get to number one has been going on for ages, and stars come and go.

CANDY STROTHER DEVORE MITCHELL

The real question is who is next?

Born and raised in Chicago; later relocating to Denver Colorado, Kerisha Crowder was witness to the joys and losses of life. She was born into a strict household where she was encouraged to dream big but work hard. With both her parents in the music industry, she was exposed to music at an early age. Music, you can say, runs in her DNA. Her mother put together several sold out concerts and events and her father had extensive equipment with his lifelong passion for music. Her great-uncle has ties to the great Natalie Cole. *The Qor* was destined for greatness. At the age of nine, Kerisha broke down a karaoke machine she spilled juice on and put it back together effortlessly before her mother noticed. By the time she was 13 years old, she was writing her own creative pieces. At the age of nineteen, she began rapping, and making beats using the music program Sonar.

As a woman rapper it is twice as hard. Female rappers must sell records without selling their soul. Of course, the industry is filled with sex and overindulgence. Breaking into the rap game is more than just having talent. "It takes grit, hard work, and money," CEO of *Ames Productions* explains.

"I had to study *The Qor's* craft and speak with DJ's and help her with getting noticed." After a few shows and hits, *The Qor* finally got her break. She toured with *afon.com* and rocked the mic across the United States. She was blessed with many gifts: sound engineering, video editor, photography, song writing, and spitting hot 16s - just to name some of the skills she boasts. She considers herself a trendsetter and has worked with several heavy hitters in the music industry. Antonette Ames, of *Ames Productions*, remembers *The Qor's* humble beginnings.

"I recall her working out of the closet in her apartment and her photos in front of her shower curtains.

I see the growth."

The debut album she created titled, *I Gotta Have It*, has been released. It is available for download and online streaming from all major streaming services like *Google Play*, *iTunes*, *Soundcloud*, *Spotify*, etc. She is currently preparing to head back on tour with *Ames Productions* in a six-city tour. With more projects in the works, you can bet your last dollar, *The Qor* will be a household name very soon.

With great lyrics, attention to detail, and down to earth personality, it's her time to shine!

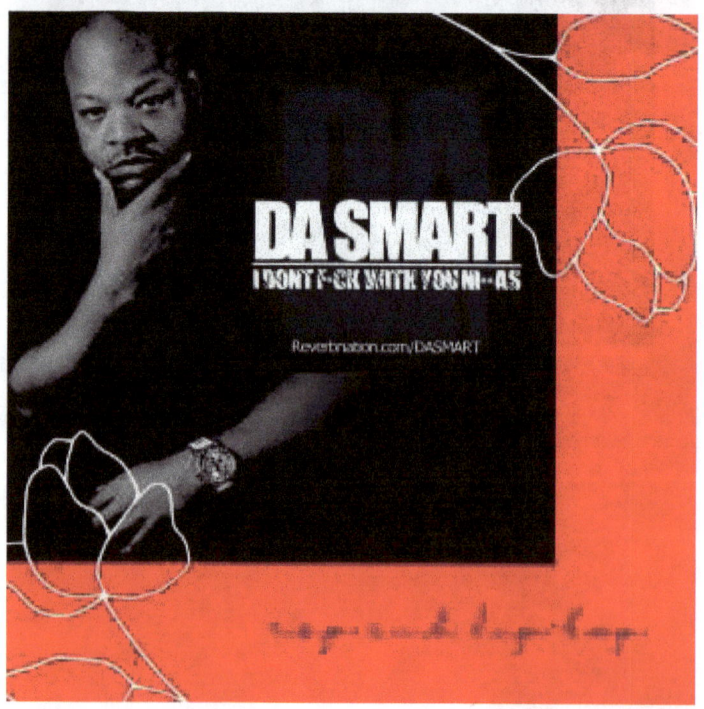

FACES OF RAP MOTHERS – BOOK FOUR

WWW.FACESOFRAPMOTHERS.COM

"It ain't no fun if the homies can't have none."
Snoop Dogg

RAP MOTHER

ANTONETTE AMES

WWW.FACESOFRAPMOTHERS.COM

CHAPTER THREE

DIANNA BOSS

CANDY STROTHER DEVORE MITCHELL

Dianna grew up in South Los Angeles as the youngest child of four siblings. Dianna feels her life has been truly blessed. She had a blessed childhood with a kind loving mother as her mother's only daughter having three brothers.

Dianna Boss met me, Candy Strother DeVore Mitchell, thirty years ago in Hollywood through her brother T-Bone Reed who was a very popular dancer. T-Bone is widely known throughout Los Angeles. She watched her brother, T-Bone dance with the famous dance group, Robot Boys in Hollywood and when he performed on Soul Train and other dance music programs. He starred with Snoop Dogg's, *Murder Was The Case That She Gave Me* and on Will.I.Am's *Insomiac* music video.

Dianna enjoys being a *Faces of Rap Mothers* member. Currently, she is the Chief Executive Officer (CEO) of the *Faces of Rap Mothers Television Network* and is a member of the *Faces of Rap Mothers Music Group* where she performs on the remake of "Goodies" originally by Ciara. Also on "Touch My Body" remake of Mariah Carey's song, which is being voiced over by rap mother Angela Gilchrist-Guyton. Over the years, Candy and Dianna, developed a close bond, which led to Dianna being a trusted source to Mrs. DeVore-Mitchell in her entrepreneurial endeavors.

Due to her strong association with Candy, Dianna has been included in multiple *Faces of Rap Mothers* books through *Beat Deep Books Imprint* of DonnaInk *Publications, L.L.C.* where rap mother Ms. Donna L. Quesinberry is Candy's publisher; also in varied magazines, such as Mark Rowe's *Soul Central* and Tyrese Gibson's sister Queen G's, *Let's Go To Work Entertainment* who created a special edition for the *Faces of Rap Mothers* alongside their Book Two publication As a result of *Faces of Rap Mothers*, Ms. Boss is making friends with genuine rap and hip hop superstar celebrities, while remaining a supportive business-woman working with the Candy and other members in building *Faces of Rap Mothers,* a California corporation doing business (dba) as *Faces of Rap Mothers Enterprise.*

As an advocate for foster children, supporting adoption, she serves children and human rights and loves working toward achieving goals relative to the future *Faces of Rap Mothers Enterprise 501 (c)3* for charitable gift-giving to families in need.

Since becoming a rap mother and member, Dianna has starred in two movies that aired on MJOwn Network and on *Faces of Rap Mothers*

Television Network on Roku TV with credit to Candy Strother DeVore-Mitchell and Paper Boy *Go Getta Entertainment* as a reality star. Both Candy Strother DeVore Mitchell and Dianna Boss are featured on DJ Craig EC of 100.9 The Heat in Los Angeles.

Ms. Boss is honored her likeness is featured alongside other rap mothers on *Unofficial Faces of Rap Mothers* shoes and shoe boxes created by Ms. Sharon Lynette-Young and her family's private brand. She is VERY excited her daughter Reanna joined vocal *Group X*, which Mrs. DeVore-Mitchell's daughter HONEY started.

In 2022, Dianna looks forward to more advocacy work. Her intention is to spread positivity from *Faces of Rap Mothers*, and "now", rap fathers, *Enterprise* to children and youth residing in group homes. Her message is **positivity** and remaining in school through a commitment to stay on the right track and working hard toward life goal setting and achievement. Ms. Boss wants to touch deep subjects such as combating teenage pregancy, having been a child mom herself, with her first child born at fifteen-years of age.

The greatest thing to happen to rap mother Dianna Boss in year of 2020 was becoming a *Faces of Rap Mothers Member*, actress, and now, vocalist where the television network provides an additiional platform for sharing positive advocacy messages. The Faces of Rap Mothers Television Network is aired worldwide on Roku, Amazon Firestick and Apple TV with PPV on Muuzictyme.com.

Ms. Dianna Boss remains grateful to Candy Strother DeVore Mitchell, *Faces of Rap Mothers* owner and to her Heavenly Father. As well she extends a big thank you to all the rap mothers and rap fathers who continue in support while working to build the *Enterprise.*

She extends a special thanks to her older brother hip hop dancer T-Bone Reed who Candy shares many fond memories with her good friend Candy Strother DeVore-Mitchell, who is the reason she became a *Faces of Rap Mothers Enterprise Member Artist.*

CANDY STROTHER DEVORE MITCHELL

FACES OF RAP MOTHERS – BOOK FOUR

*Donna*Ink Publications, L.L.C. | *Beat Deep Books Copyright Protected*

CANDY STROTHER DEVORE MITCHELL

FACES OF RAP MOTHERS – BOOK FOUR

CHAPTER FOUR

TINA BROWN

BROUGHT INTO MY LIFE BY OUR HEAVENLY Father God is my god sister Tina Brown. Unforgettable Tina. That is what I call her. One day with Ms. Lady Tina Brown and you have an amazing memory for life. Tina has an unforgettable personality. Everyone is drawn to her like cats are drawn to milk. She is sensitive and exciting. I am loving being with Tina Brown, it is like an amusement park ride on one of the craziest rollercoasters. Tina also shares a deep sense of humor.

Born to Herbert and Carole Brown, Tina has three sisters (i.e.: Bethy, Lele, and Carole) and two brothers (i.e.: Tommy and Bobby). She also has one half-brother.

Her brother Bobby Brown is a world-famous superstar as one of the members of New Edition. He is also a Grammy winning superstar and solo artist with a string of Number 1 hits known as the *King of Stage*.

Tina is also the sister-in-law to one of the most famous beautiful voices in the world, a Superstar Queen Diva, who was world famous, Whitney Houston. Tina Brown is an aunt to Whitney Houston and Bobby Brown's daughter Bobby Kristina Houston-Brown. Like all her siblings, Tina assisted her brother Bobby and Whitney Houston with caring for and raising their Princess Bobby Kristina Houston-Brown. She traveled the world with Whitney and Bobby including Israel, Africa, and other countries. There is no place on the planet that Tina Brown has not been to. She has met, and dined, with world famous celebrities and African royals along with her with her sister-in-law Whitney and her brother Bobby.

As a mother in her own right, Tina has six beautiful children (e.g.: three boys and three girls). She has a host of grandchildren and raised numerous children who call her mom to whom she did not give birth.

Tina's legacy is to be remembered as a spokesperson and motivational speaker. She passes a positive message to youth worldwide to stay in school and at home with parental guidance. If possible, she tells young people to get a higher education while remaining on the right track in life because not doing so has costs and she shares those costs are not worthwhile. Instead, choose the right path to success.

FACES OF RAP MOTHERS – BOOK FOUR

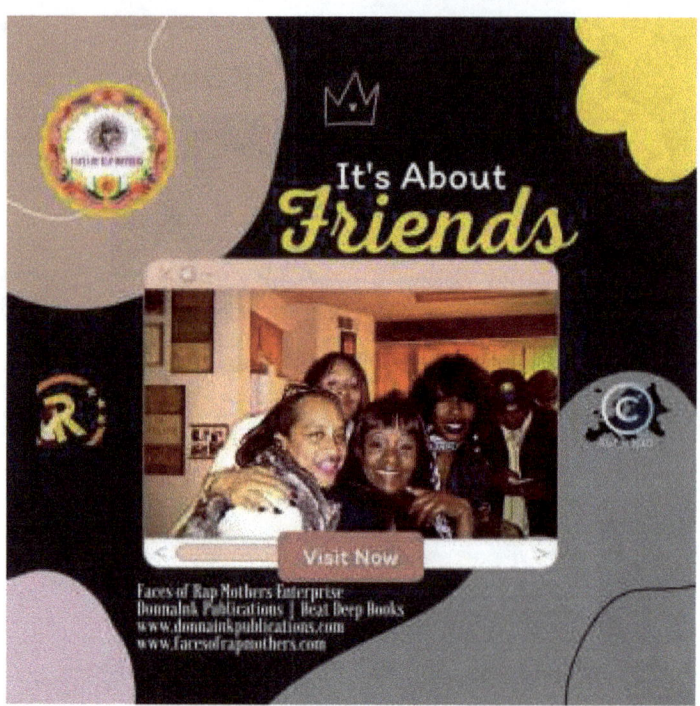

CHAPTER FIVE

CARLENE CORSEY

C ARLENE CORSEY IS CURRENTLY AIRING ON the *Faces of Rap Mothers Television Network*. She has been studying writing and is developing her first script for her "first" movie titled, 42nd Place, which conveys the story of growing up with her grandmother and sharing "family on the porch" moments.

The one-shot film, "A Familiar Lie", which Carlene is in released in 2020 about a devoted wife who suspects her husband is having an affair and after hiring a private investigator to learn more – discovers more than she desires to know. The movie stars Omar Gooding and Trae Ireland among others – Corsey plays herself.

Carlene has "one" son, King. Apart from acting and writing, she strives to help those less fortunate. She also enjoys watching her favorite YouTubers and stays busy promoting her own projects and supporting her son King's celebrity hair style business. Additionally, she stays prayed up to best advantage each day while growing and developing into a better person each day. Carlene's acting credits include:

- 2021: *Blunt News* – as Hooker
- 2021: *A Familiar Lie 2: Niggas & Flies* (pre-production) - as Carlene Corsey
- 2020: *A Familiar Lie* – as Carlene Corsey
- 2019: South Central Love – as Mama Dee
- 2019: *Cycles in Love* (Short) – as Amanda
- 2019: *7th and Westlake: Nino's Revenge* – as Boscee
- 2018: *Loyalty* (Short) – as Mama Dee
- 2017: *Avenge the Crows - Gangsta Girl in Park* (uncredited)
- 2013: *America's Court with Judge Ross (TV Series)* – as Yvonne Martin
- Etc. with more to come

CARLENE CORSEY
Actress / Host

Height: 5'2 Weight: 105
Eyes: Brown Hair: Brown

ADDRESS
Los Angeles, CA

PHONE
213 590 8845

EMAIL
carlenecorseypr@gmail.com

CREDITS

2019
KINGS SOLE (EXECT. PRODUCER & LINE PRODUCER)

2019
SOUTH CENTRAL LOVE (MAMA DEE)

2019
CYCLES IN LOVE SHORT (AMANDA)

2018
LOYALTY SHORT (MAMA DEE)

2017
AVENGE THE CROWS (GANGSTA GIRL)

2013
AMERICA'S COURT
JUDGE ROSS (YVONNE MARTIN)

TRAINING

1998-1999 JOHN R. POWERS (COMMERCIALS)
2006-2008 SOUTHWEST COLLEGE (THEATER)
2015-2016 RMCONAIR RADIO ST. (PODCAST)

ABOUT ME

I love reading and helping others by giving words of encouragement. I'm a mother with one son whose the light of my life. My goal is to become self sufficient putting myself in position to open doors for others. I'm very energetic, free spirit and ambitious. I host my own live TV show " Global Street Wave " offering interviews and speaking on real life topics.

SPECIAL SKILLS

I am a born natural when it comes to Acting I've been told and I have shown it as well. I am easy to work with and a great listener. I catch on quick and also can assist to help any task get fulfilled. I can do the work and deliver exceptional results. I possess a combination of skills and experience that make me stand out.

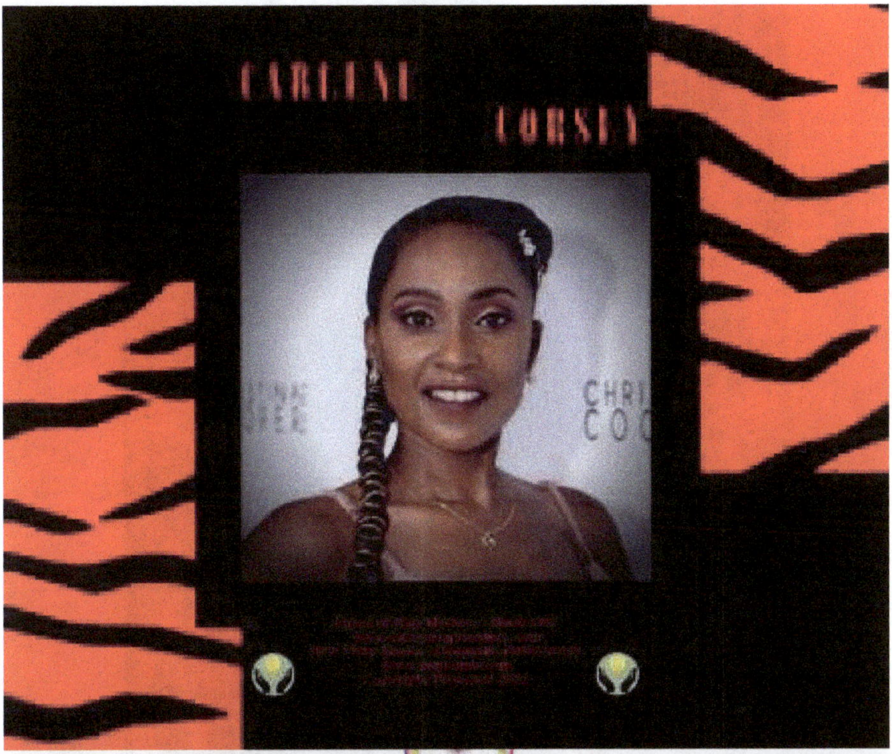

FACES OF RAP MOTHERS
Book Two
CANDY STROTHER
DEVORE MITCHELL

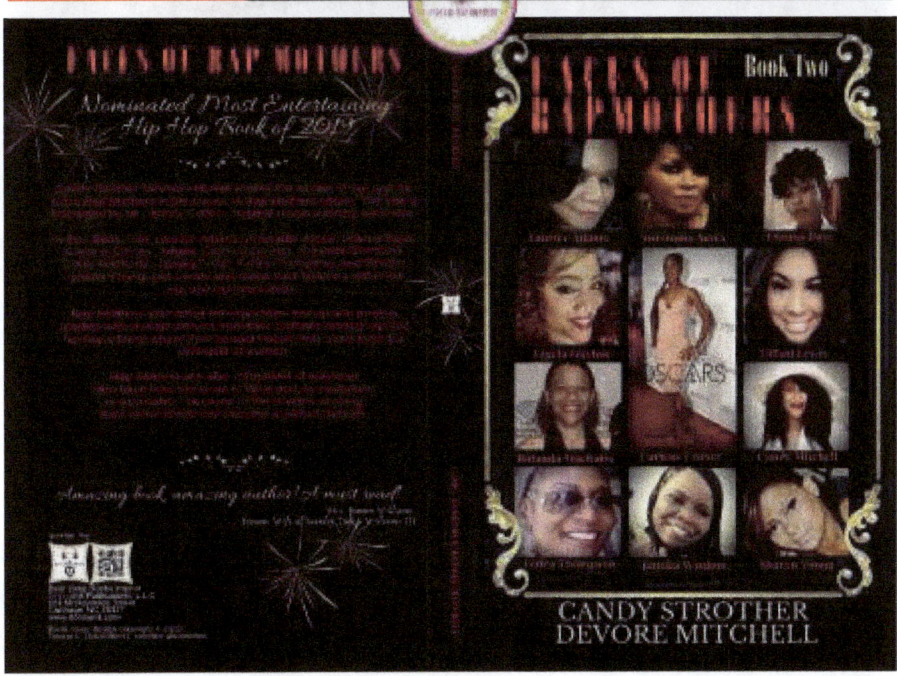

FACES OF RAP MOTHERS – BOOK FOUR

CHAPTER SIX

THERESA FORD

CANDY STROTHER DEVORE MITCHELL

Theresa Ford is known for her work on:

Theresa Ford
Actress (6)

BabyGirl
(Short)
Gussie

Family Reunion
(TV Series 2019-2020)
Sister Carter (2 episodes, 2019-2020)

Ledisi: Add to Me
(Short 2017)
Party Guest

HeadShop
Church Member

Lawd Have Mercy
(TV Series 2017)
Church Hag / Choir Member (11 episodes, 2017)

House Arrest
(2012/I)
Choir Member

Theresa Ford

Self (1)

Love on A Two Way Street
(TV Special 2020)

Hildee

To learn more about Ms. Ford, visit *Faces of Rap Mothers Television Network* on Roku or our social featured in *Faces of Rap Mothers Book Four* back matter. Also, consider these sites:

CANDY STROTHER DEVORE MITCHELL

Theresa Ford
BOOKED IT

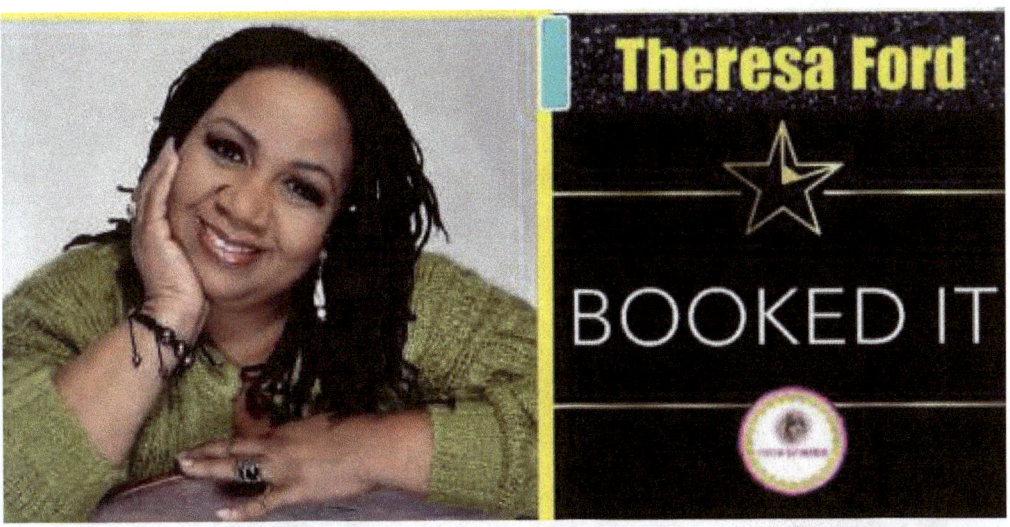

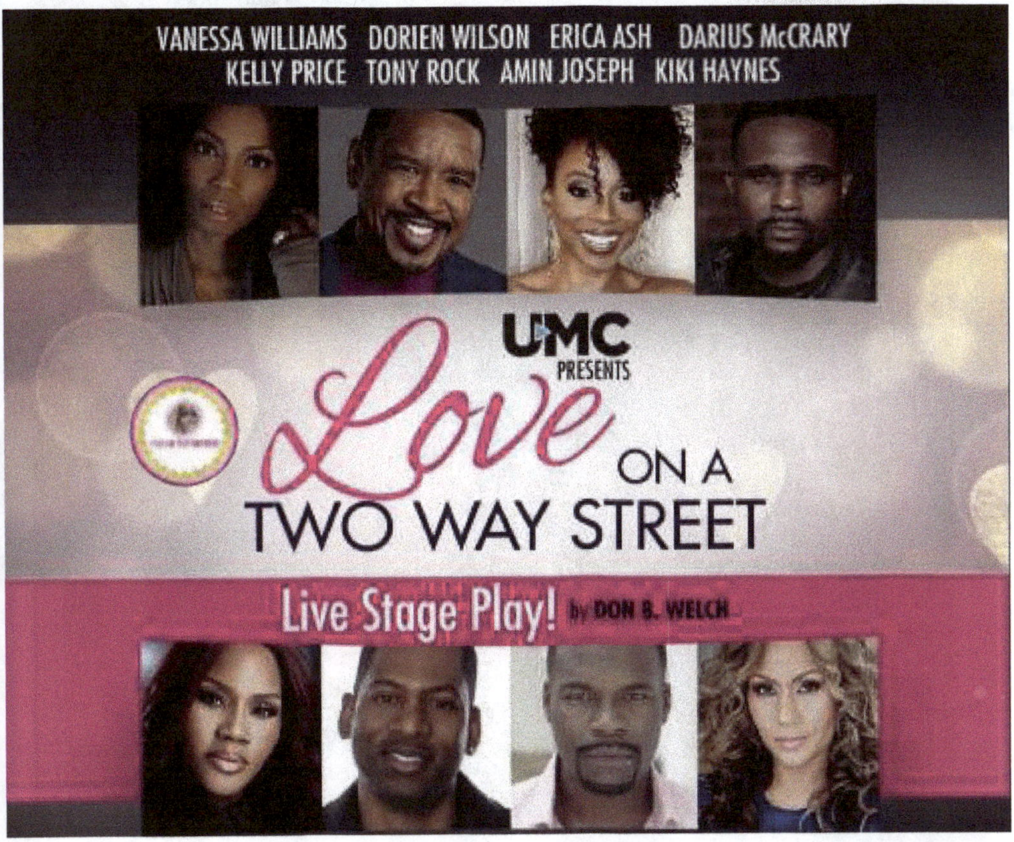
VANESSA WILLIAMS DORIEN WILSON ERICA ASH DARIUS McCRARY
KELLY PRICE TONY ROCK AMIN JOSEPH KIKI HAYNES
UMC
PRESENTS
Love
ON A
TWO WAY STREET
Live Stage Play! by DON B. WELCH

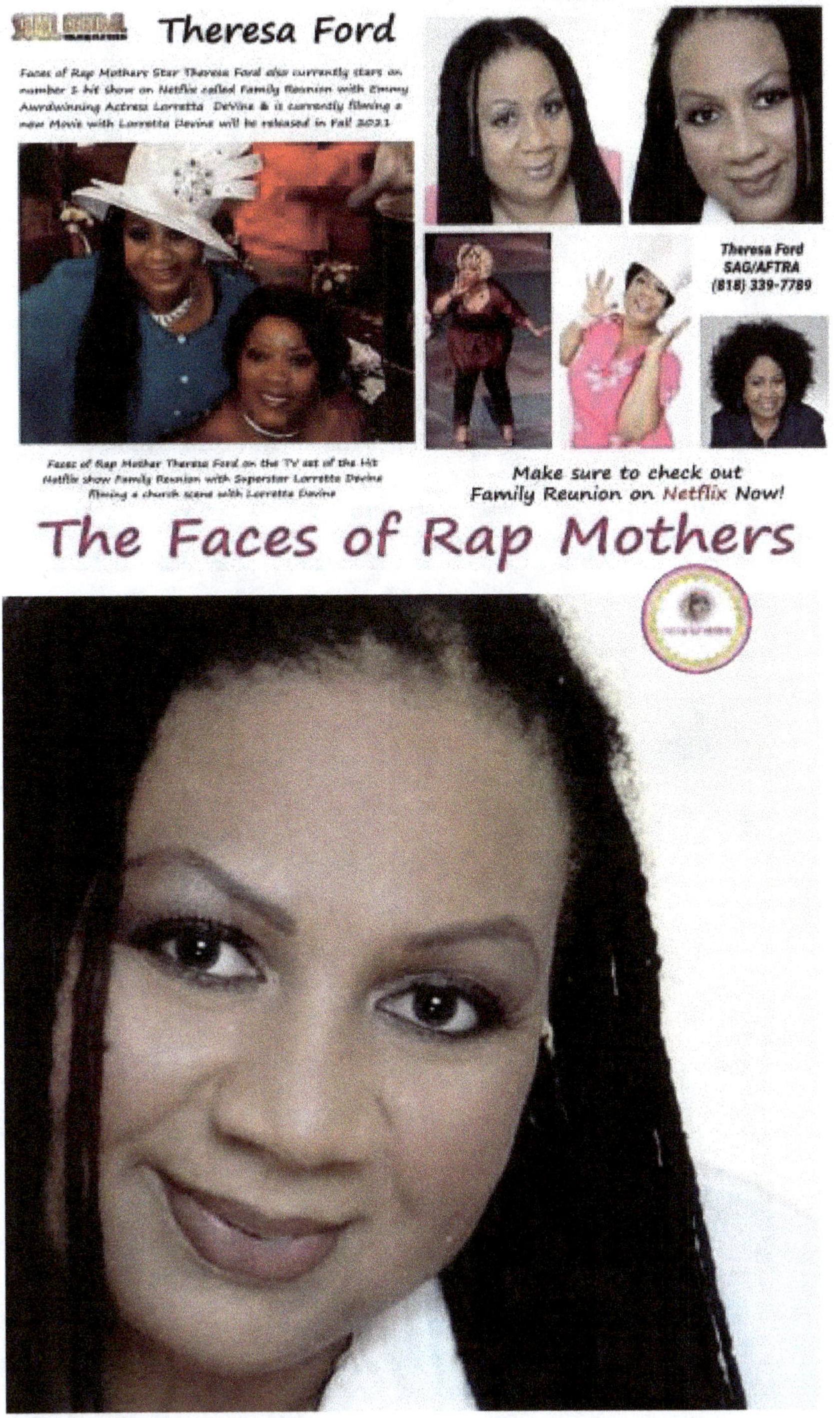

FACES OF RAP MOTHERS – BOOK FOUR

The Faces of Rap Mothers

CANDY STROTHER DEVORE MITCHELL

FACES OF RAP MOTHERS – BOOK FOUR

CHAPTER SEVEN

QUEEN G
SHONTA GIBSON

CANDY STROTHER DEVORE MITCHELL

*F*aces of Rap Mothers – Book Four, shares the Shonta Renee Gibson, better known as "Queen G", story. One of my best friends, Queen G has shared my titles generously. Her love for my brand and company continues to bring the *Faces of Rap Mothers Enterprise* message to readers around the country. Associates who are willing to risk it all to share your work can provide a wealth of abundance and Queen G's novel ideas and inspirations have continued to impact all the *Faces of Rap Mothers* book series and for this, I am grateful – due to same, Queen G is a Vice President on the *Faces of Rap Mothers Television Network*. Thank you, Queen!

About Shonta Renee Gibson "Queen G":

Shonta Renee Gibson, better known in the rap and hip-hop community as, "Queen G" is best known for her work as a blogger, entertainment writer, and interviewer with a career that has spanned twenty years in doing she loves. In 2016, Queen G's life took a detour when she traveled to Las Vegas from Los Angeles. Being very tired, having been up all-night doing hair for LA clients, Queen G heard an inner voice believing God wanted her to get home quickly. Under severe fatigue, she followed that voice and arrived at home to a loving family happy for her return who greeted her with open arms. As she began making dinner for her husband and children, it was about 113 degrees – the weather was unusually hot.

"Anyone who knows Vegas, knows the heat shares a distinction relative to hell," Queen G professes. "My husband stepped outside to smoke in a pair of shorts - he took one puff and immediately came back indoors." When Queen G glimpsed at her husband - he plopped down in a lounge chair with no bodily control.

She saw his face slump before her eyes. As he attempted to mouth the words, "I love you," his speech slurred. It was as if he had been at the dentist and received numbing medication. Holding him up in the lounge chair, Queen G acted fast and dialed 911. About seven minutes later an ambulance arrived but it felt like hours, she states, "It was very scary."

When the Emergency Management System (EMS) looked at her husband, they identified he was having a stroke and transported him to the emergency ward for treatment. In the upcoming days, this reality proved challenging for her family due to an uncertainty regarding recovery. It took some time. However, Queen G's husband did recover but could no longer work in extreme heat and subsequently lost his job. It was then, the nightmare of homelessness began. Shortly after his release from the hospital - the family was evicted. For the first time, there was not a "solid plan" regarding where to go, or what to do, for their family. In shock, but still an entertainer at heart, Queen G had the sensibility to know keeping their situation private would be a wise familial decision.

With four children, her family's life was packed into the family vehicle and while the couple had friends for a week or two overnight stays, they had little resources to work with. Her husband's newfound inability to work was not easy on either of them as parents and even more difficult to address to the children.

"Asking for help was an extremely humbling experience," Queen G recollects. With limited programs for homeless families in Vegas, hotel vouchers took some time and effort to acquire. Asking for help from the county was nearly impossible – at every impasse a lengthy process was required and when unable to get a hotel room her family had to sleep in the car. When an income kicked back in – it afforded a modest weekly kitchenette – a breath of fresh air but not like home. When their money depleted and folks, they knew who were willing to help, tapped out, Queen G, her husband and their children lived on a wing and a prayer relying on God and their faith to keep them going. It was a nightmare, which seemed as if it would not end.

Queen G felt the torture of desperation without a solid presentation for their children and this broke her heart but despite all that – her husband and her managed to keep their children in school. This meant four different schools within brief time frames while moving around and homeless. It drained everyone emotionally and many mornings Queen G and her husband washed their babies in a gas station restroom for their school preparation and combed their hair in the back seat of the family vehicle; however, they overcame it all.

Queen G Shares an Inspirational Message:

"I wasn't going to allow my children to fail in their education even though we felt like failures as parents. On one afternoon, walking through Molasky Park and thinking about our situation, I spotted a beautiful couple who were also homeless. They appeared not to allow their circumstances to get to them. I stopped to speak with them because the entire time I was homeless, I still interviewed for entertainment programs – my instincts were always investigative.

"While talking to the couple and hearing their story, a voice spoke to me and stated, "Look around." I glanced around the park noticing many people in our predicament – also homeless. The voice spoke to me again, "This is your mission - feed my people in this park." At that moment, I was unaware of how I could possibly feed people who were not able to manage, when we could not manage for ourselves. I knew I could not go against the voice I had heard, which I believe was a voice from God.

"In the following month, while still living in a weekly, my husband and I obeyed the prompting I had received. We cooked spaghetti and banana pudding and prepped rolls and salad and managed some bottled water. We wanted to share meals we ourselves would eat. We said a prayer before taking the food to the park to serve to the homeless. In the next month two additional volunteers joined us and by the next month four volunteers joined, then fourteen, then forty-two . . . the vision grew exponentially rapidly.

"As we continued providing food service - we started filming and photographing our experiences for distribution on social media. We filmed documentaries about homelessness under the Las Vegas tunnels – it was incredible and life changing. Together we learned through the process and held compassion for the people we served.

"We formalized the mission and titled it, *Operation Bring Your Best*. As volunteers increased in volume, we were providing clothes, groceries, shoes, toiletries, etc. to the homeless. The operation became an enormous success and the homeless began to depend on us. It touched my heart seeing people helped through our mission.

"*DJ Thump* from Vegas took notice of our mission and booked me as his first *Community Spotlight guest on Power 88*. His radio program aired mornings and prime time. *DJ Remixx* also showed us love on his Sunday radio mix as well. Soul Central and *On The Rise Magazine* spotlighted us too. In months that followed I was awarded, *Sister of the*

Year from Minister Stretch at a huge community festival, which was a great honor.

"Through our mission I learned life belongs to a higher power and that following my inner voice or "spirit" is essential to my progression. I grew to understand our life changes and when it does, we must trust in the process, and trust in the Lord. Our homeless nightmare turned into a calling and now I believe everything happens for a reason. Our homelessness lasted an entire year and when we did get into a new home, I had to pinch myself as I could not believe it was real. Our family passed a life test arriving at a new life mission while remaining solid and that is as good as it gets."

Currently, for *Faces of Rap Mothers Enterprise*, Shonta Renee Gibson is Vice President and Programmer on *Faces of Rap Mothers Television Network*.

FACES OF RAP MOTHERS – BOOK FOUR

CANDY STROTHER DEVORE MITCHELL

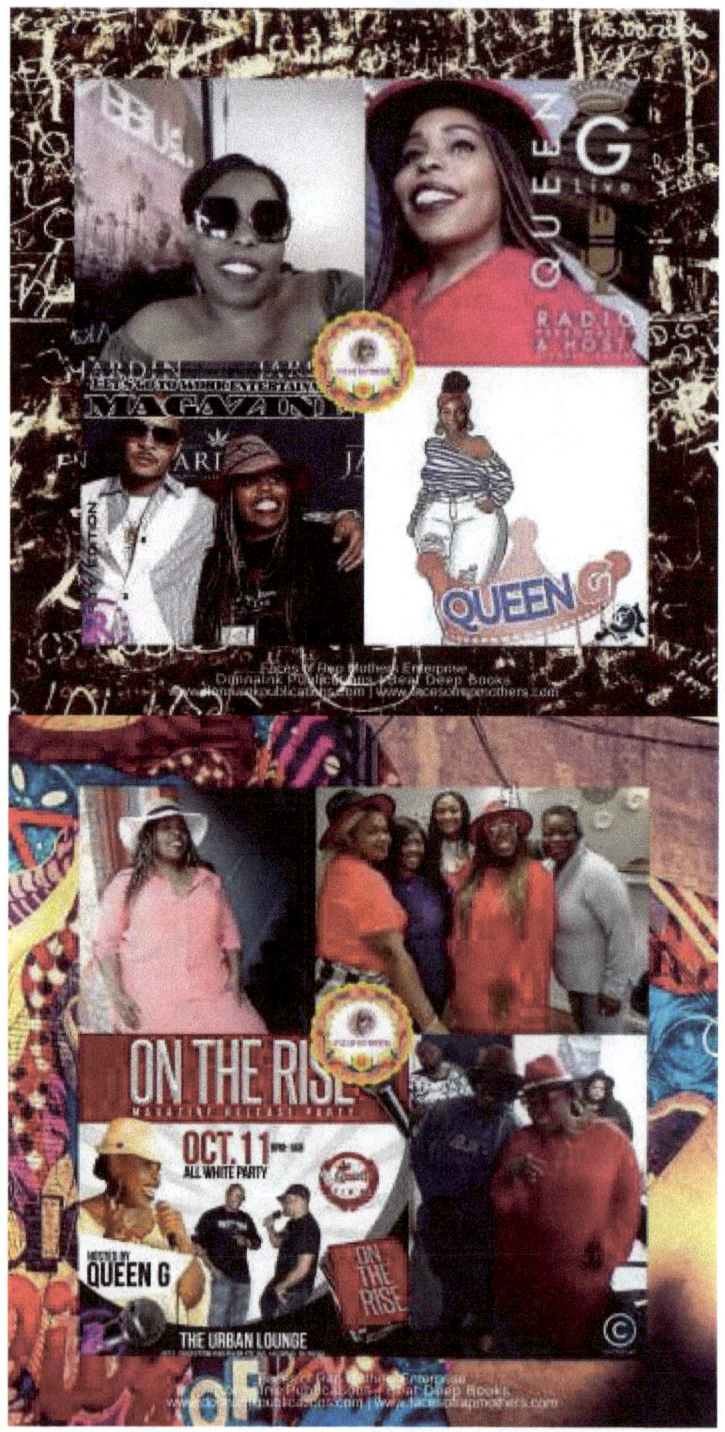

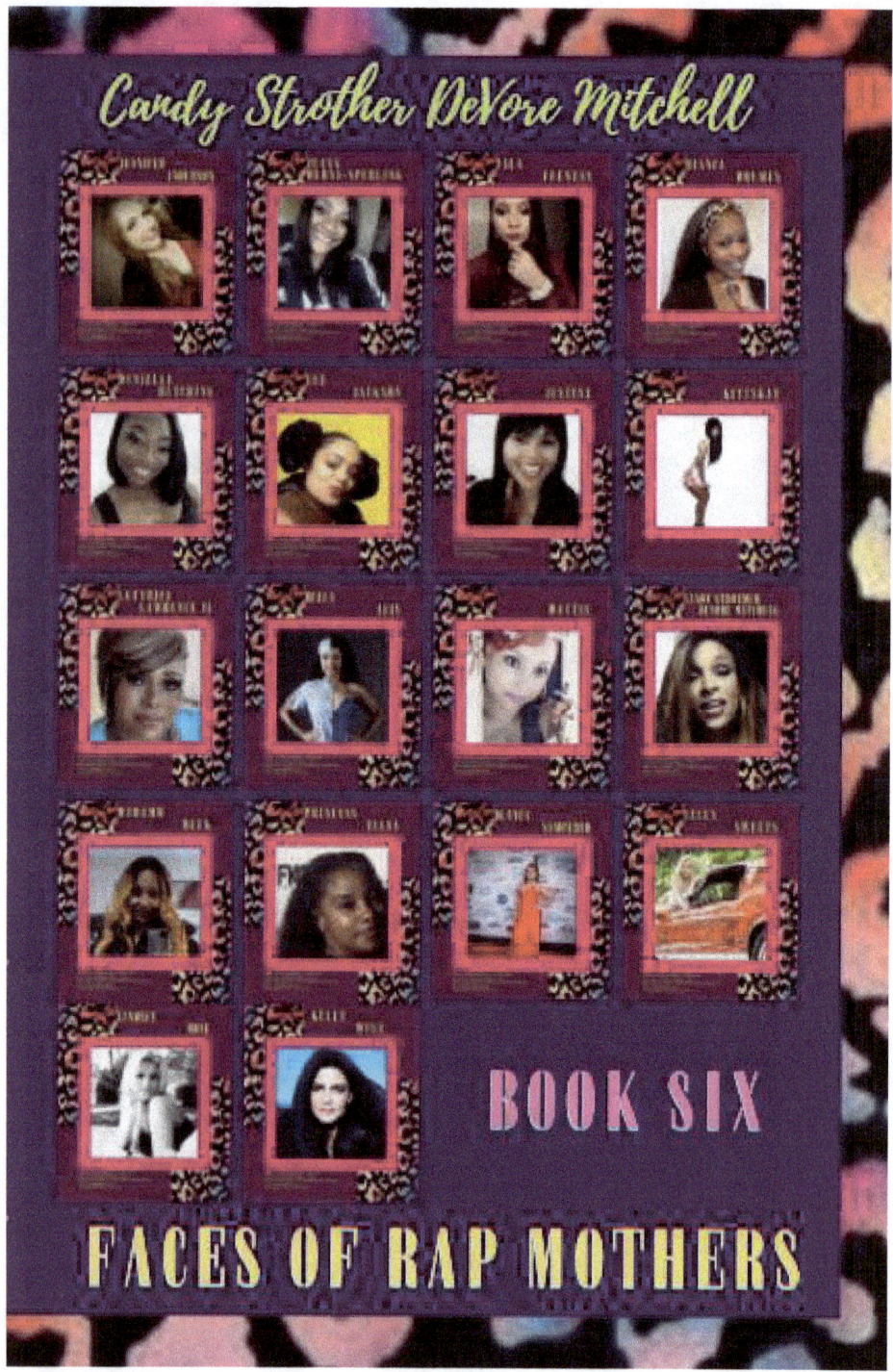

CHAPTER EIGHT

MARIAH JERIDO

CANDY STROTHER DEVORE MITCHELL

CEO, AUTHOR, MODEL, SONGWRITER, Magazine-Editor-In-Chief, Photographer, Public-Speaker, and Network Owner Mariah Marie Jerido was born 28 May 1964 in Florence South Carolina. She was raised in Jersey City, New Jersey, as an infant for half of her childhood. Today, Mariah considers herself a city and country girl.

After her father's death, at six years of age, when her Daddy was twenty-five - Mariah's mother decided to raise her and her siblings in South Carolina in Mayesville. The town was in the country and where Ms. Jerido attended school. Mariah's style turns heads of many people - even children who admire her pretty smile – since being a child, she dreamed of being known around the world as a leader helping others and is considered a talented woman reaching her peak of popularity with rapid progress.

Upon graduation Mayewood High School in 1982, Mariah moved away from the small-town life and began her life journey. First moving to Florence SC where she was born and later traveling to Washington DC metropolitan area in Capitol Heights Maryland. She resided there for seven years and in 1991 decided to make her permanent home in Queen City . . . Charlotte NC.

In Charlotte is where Mariah's life began that life changed her forever. Rising above mediocrity – on 24 May 2003 just four days prior to her birthday (28 May) Mariah had a near-death car accident and was thrown out of the car headfirst resulting in a coma, which she awakened from two months later in July of 2003. The accident and subsequent trauma left her scarred for life wondering if her dreams were over.

Ten years later, Mariah followed the spirit - keeping hope alive with a faith in God and herself. In her own words, "I wanted more than what people Charlotte N.C. could offer. I felt I had outgrown the city and it was beginning to bother me; over the years I had branded myself as a future-seeker, so after twenty-eight years why give up?"

With a sociable lifestyle, good reputation, and respectable career – Mariah knew her performance excellence in any, and everything, she approached career-wise came to bear. For twenty-eight years she dedicated herself to Charlotte N.C. and helped people achieve their goals and dreams.

Well-known as Ms. Pecan in Charlotte within the entertainment industry; Mariah decided to move on – since 18 August 2013 she has resided in Atlanta Georgia where she is actively pursuing her dreams while praying for a breakthrough to change her life and the many people she can reach within the world. Her goal of accomplishing bigger ambitions began to push her forward away from Charlotte to Atlanta where her vision for her career came true.

By reaching the decision to give up everything she owned, her beautiful home, cars, antiques - even leaving close friends and family behind – Mariah reached her desired outcome. There were challenging times, struggles, trails, tribulations, and difficulties on her journey. But she believed through overcoming her traumatic brain injury (TBI) as a survivor – she would endure it all.

And on the journey, she did the unthinkable and went to college. With a TBI and memory issues, going to college was a challenge; however, Mariah knew it would aid her in making her dreams come true as a photographer. She enrolled in *The Arts Institute of Atlanta Georgia*, 19 August 2013, and never will forget it. She became homeless on the first day of school in Atlanta, which was shocking. Having no idea where she would lay her head that afternoon after school, she planned to sleep in her car so she could be in school the next day on time. She was determined and while each day featured a trial and tribulation – Mariah made step-by-step progress to complete a truly remarkable journey.

Her heart centered on producing a healing show and she developed the web series, *Beautiful by Jerido* (e.g.: majestic role models with flaws). Her program is currently in the making for upcoming web / reality television viewing. Her show started as a dream over thirteen years earlier due to her accident and the pains of life and over the years, while building and branding herself – even learning to read, spell, and write again never diminished her belief in success.

Beautiful By Jerido (MRMWF) became a project one year later while attending The Art Institute of Atlanta. Mariah's Jerido Productions LLC company came together after fourteen years of dreaming how to bring things to reality to aid ordinary people like herself with healing while turning their lives around – basically achieving *Beautifully Flawed Women and Men Role Models*.

Mariah realized it hers were not easy dreams – but she never gave up. Once she realized her dream realizes this needs to be shared with the public and how the dream is going to become a WebTV series and the Reality show Project was planned. The series follows a group of women and men from all over sharing Testimonies about their dreams, goals, Trials, and Tribulations of life pains and obstacles. A legacy was made to help people. In the spring 2020 divine timing happened for Mariah's to have her own network and the dreams just got bigger and bigger she said and now today Mariah is the CEO of her own network that is **MJ OWN NETWORK!** all Mariah's shows are being on her own network TV Channel on ROKU to start and in the future and looking forward to owning more channels. The rest is history!

Mariah Jerido Motto In her own words: "America Is the Land Of Opportunity" My company wants to help support that motto, by fulfilling people's dreams who always wanted to be all they can be in the Entertainment Industry. I happen to believe that there is no competition in the industry, only hard work, right marketing, skills in the delivery of a performance, strategic placement of a finished work and maximization of audience acceptability, and then, the final ingredient. The audience is like a big pie. Somewhere in that pie are those who will like what we do. It should not matter how we look, our age or race. All we must do is satisfy them and we can enjoy our piece of the pie. The only one we are in competition within this world is Ourselves.

The business! **JERIDO PRODUCTIONS LLC / MJ OWN NETWORK** Is an Entertainment | Multimedia | Film and Studio Production Company that is committed to providing entertainment for the network, a Worldwide Audience and Diverse Audiences. The Business! **JERIDO PRODUCTIONS / MJ OWN NETWORK** is Building a LEGACY and NETWORK PLATFORM for the FUTURE of ENTERTAINMENT. MJ OWN NETWORK strives to bring the best out of all people. Now one of "The Faces of Rap Mothers" brings joy to Mariah's life and is honored to have it on MJ OWN NETWORK.

Mariah's own words: I remind myself every day I am Unstoppable, Courageous and a Phenomenal woman who is a woman on the move never giving up and I will always devote myself to helping others.

FACEBOOK:	https://www.facebook.com/mjownnetwork
INSTAGRAM:	https://www.instagram.com/mjownnetwork
LINKEDIN:	https://www.linkedin.com/in/mjownnetwork
TWITTER:	https://twitter.com/mjownnetwork
WEBSITE:	https://www.mjownnetwork.com
YOUTUBE:	https://www.mjownnetwork.com

CANDY STROTHER DEVORE MITCHELL

CHAPTER TEN

TERESA KEMP

TERESA R. KEMP – 5th GENERATION QUILTER, Military Historian, Owner of the *UGRR Quilt Code Museum Collections & Plantation Quilts*, Ms. Kemp was born in Baumholder, West Germany to the late Dr. Howard and Serena Strother-Wilson. She graduated from Berlin American High School and attended Ohio State University (OSU) in Columbus, OH. She transferred to West Virginia State University (WVSU), graduating with her Bachelor of Arts (BA) degree. Kemp also received her Bachelor of Science (BS) degree in Computer Information Systems from DeVry University, Atlanta, GA. As a computer programmer analyst, Teresa worked for Georgia Pacific in shared accounting taxes / controllers, writing financial software and performing enterprise security administration.

In 2005 to 2007, Ms. Kemp, alongside her parents, opened the *UGRR Secret Quilt Code Museum* in Underground Atlanta. In 2015, Teresa opened *SC Wild's Heritage Center* in McCormick SC's 108 yr.-old *McCormick Train Depot*. Currently, she is appearing on *Faces of Rap Mother's Television Network* for the weekly learning portal historic segment and on the *International Online Hip Hop Museum*.

Ms. Kemp has successfully fought colon cancer and subsequent congestive heart failure to "Keep the Show on the Road". The great-granddaughter of a South Carolina plantation owner, David R. Strother, and Ann Jones (Native American), Teresa is the descendant of African ancestors who were former slaves and abolitionists. She is passionate about documenting her diverse history. Her Strother family has several plantation homes in South Carolina that are on the *National Registry of Historic Places*.

Ms. Kemp is a modern-day researcher of international human slavery; where she preserves, and documents, worldwide cultural heritage. Her Farrow family arrived as slaves, living in coastal Georgia on the Dover Hall plantation. Listed in two wills and four slave valuements, they were freed in 1858 and feature a rare view into day-today work on plantations.

The Farrows kept their culture alive with absentee owners (6 months a year) due to malaria and yellow fever epidemics. A blacksmith Peter, and Eliza (seamstress/midwife), hired themselves out and worked on neighboring plantations. He preached in brush arbors and planned escapes. Keeping their money, their owner required a percentage of the proceeds of their labor, on return. An

Awka (itinerant metal smith), he did the same in Nigeria, teaching of Chukwu (God), arbitrating in caves, and praying for the sick. He worked and brought his money back for support of the village.

Teresa continues to transition her museum programs, classes and extensive collections and exhibits online to encourage preservation and access to international audience. A mother, grandmother and great grandmother, Ms. Kemp is a servant of the Lord Jesus Christ. She was called thirty-five years ago to teach, *Freedom through Obedience to God's Word*.

Teresa also performs rural arts and crafts as gallery activities to preserve the culture at presentations. She fights human trafficking using her exhibits to teach delayed gratification and reconciliation skills.

Visit www.PlantationQuilts.com

Teresa R. Kemp
Nana Efua Adadzewa 1st
Queen Mother Mankessim Traditional Area
Central Region, Ghana West Africa
trkemp@PlantationQuilts.com
Phone: USA +1 (803) 618-2250

Mrs. Teresa R. Kemp

Author, 5th Generation Quilter, Abolitionist, Historian, Researcher, Grant Writing Instructor, Owner of Plantation Quilts and UGRR Secret Quilt Code Museum

Born in Baumholder, West Germany to the late Dr. Howard and Serena (Strother) Wilson. She graduated from Berlin American High School and attended the Ohio State Univ. in Columbus, OH. She transferred to WV State University and graduated with a BA. She graduated from DeVry University in Decatur, GA with a BS in Computer Information Systems. As a Computer Programmer Analyst, she worked for Georgia Pacific Corporation in Shared Accounting Taxes and Controllers Office, writing financial software, and performing Enterprise-wide Security Administration. In 2005, with her parents she opened the UGRR Secret QuiltCode Museum. Teresa closed in 2007 due to illness, she has successfully fought colon cancer and congestive heart failure. She has a Project Management Certification and worked at the APEX Museum. A staunch advocate for healthier lifestyles for all, she continues to grow stronger by participating in the YMCA's "Live Strong" program. As an Abolitionist, she fights Human Trafficking while researching international slavery, documenting and preserves the world's cultural heritage. She is a grant writing instructor, and teaches entrepreneurial courses to bring economic and financial freedom to "at-risk populations and communities.

Teresa is the great-granddaughter of a South Carolina plantation owner, David R. Strother and Ann Jones (Native American woman and descendant of Peter and Eliza Farrow, her West African ancestors who were former slaves/abolitionist, she was passionate about documenting and exhibiting her diverse history. Teresa's Strother family has several plantation homes located in SC on the Nat. Register of Historic Places. Her mother was one of 17 children. Serena's father and eleven of her mother's siblings were born prior to 1900. She has copies of certified wills, photos, census data, birth, marriage, death, and military service records dating back to her first immigrant ancestor William Strother, who settled in 17th century Virginia, to share with you.

Her Farrow family came from Africa with a history documented to 1042 BC, to America as slaves, called Geechie-Gullah people, they were freed and lived in coastal GA. Listed on South Carolina's Dover Hall Plantation in 2 wills, along with 4 slave valuements and the Farrows were free by 1858. It's a rare view into day-to-day work on plantations. The Farrows, though enslaved kept their cultures with absentee owners (6 months a year) due to malaria and yellow fever epidemics. As a blacksmith Peter and his wife, Eliza (seamstress/midwife) could hire themselves out. When they worked on neighboring plantations, he would preach in brush arbors and planned and executed slave escapes. Keeping their money, they gave their owner a percentage of the proceeds of their labor when he returned. An Igbo Awka (Nigerian itinerate metal smith), he did the same in Nigeria, teaching of Chukwu (God), arbitrating in caves. He worked and would bringing the proceeds of their work back for support of the village. She became a Queen Mother in Ghana in 2015, Nana Efua Adadzewa 1st, Queen Mother of Mankessim Traditional Area Central Region of Ghana Africa.

Teresa continues to do traveling exhibits with her families' extensive collections of African, plantation artifacts and textiles to encourage preservation. She's a mother, grandmother, and great grandmother. A servant of the Lord Jesus Christ, she was called 35 years ago to teach "Freedom through Obedience to God's Word". Mrs. Kemp with her parents, the late Dr. Howard and Serena Wilson of Columbus, Ohio, have done more than several thousand presentations. She advocated for domestic violence issues, using her family's UGRR legacy to teach delayed gratification and reconciliation skills. Now booking engagements for 2020-2025 For more information, please visit us at: www.PlantationQuilts.com We do raise monies for organizations that are doing great work in our Mission: http://plantationquilts.com/mission.html

Affiliations: Day Star Tabernacle International, Royal Anthropological Institute of Great Britain and Ireland (RAI), American Quilt Society (AQS), National Quilting Association (NQA), Quilters for Christ, American Museum Association (AMA), YMCA, The Society of GA Archaeologist (SGA), NAACP, National Trust for Historic Preservation, Organization of American Historians, Historians Against Slavery, The Schomburg Center for Research in Black Culture, WVSU Alumni Association, DeVry University Alumni Association, Ohio State University Alumni Association, National Museum African-American History & Culture, (NMAAHC), Tuskegee Airmen Association, Inc., United States Tennis Association (USTA), Honorary Member of Brown Sugar Stitchers, Drayton Hall Historical Society, Researcher-National Archives, Atlanta History Center.

For Fees & Scheduling info:
E-mail: trkemp@PlantationQuilt.com or call (803) 618-2250.
She is Building Bridges & Keeping the Show on the Road!

CONTACT US

I would love to hear your questions, comments, and opinions.

On Line:

- Blog Spot: http://UGRRQuiltCode.BlogSpot.com
- Email: trkemp@PlantationQuilts.com
- Facebook Book Page: www.facebook.com/ugrrquiltmuseum
-
- Google+: trkemp
- LinkedIn: Mrs. Teresa R. Kemp
- Twitter: @UGRRQuiltMuseum
- Twitter: @Trfkemp
- Website: www.PlantationQuilts.com
- Youtube.com Teresa R. Kemp Keeper of the Fire

Phone: USA By phone: Country Code 001 (803) 618-2250

We have created unique programs for:

- Educational Television Programs, Podcast
- Business/Governments/Professional Associations
- Social Clubs/Churches/At-Risk Populations/Quilt Guilds
- Corporate "Lunch and Learns"/Team Building/ Diversity
- Libraries/Museums/Archives/Conference Centers
- Fraternities/Sororities/School/Family Reunions
- Colleges/Universities/Schools, Home School Associations, K-12
    Grade appropriate state requirements, hands on, interactive/Scalable Exhibits
- Community Centers / Camps/
- After-School Programs/ Home School Scholars/Research Centers
- Medical Associations/Health Fairs/ Community Programs/
- Book Clubs /Writer Associations
- Rites of Passage/Juneteenth Celebrations/Festivals/State Fairs

Video: https://www.wjbf.com/news/mccormick-county-programs-help-at-risk-youth/

"We Have Chosen Education as a Bridge to Understanding"

FACES OF RAP MOTHERS – BOOK FOUR

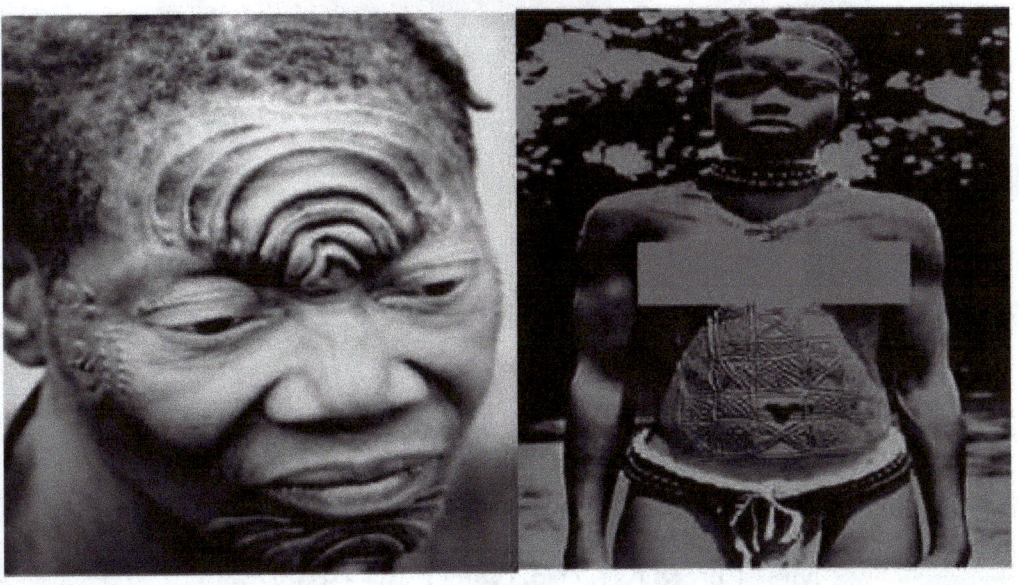

mages are subject to copyrights for more information or permission to use these photos contact
Teresa R. Kemp

CANDY STROTHER DEVORE MITCHELL

Mrs. Teresa R. Kemp, Nana Efua Adadzewa 1st
Queen Mother of Mankessim Traditional Area
Central Region of Ghana Africa

Author, 5th Generation Quilter, Abolitionist, Historian, Researcher,
Grant Writing Instructor, Owner of Plantation Quilts & UGRR Secret Quilt Code Museum
www.PlantationQuilts.com
For information on Traveling Exhibits,
Appearances Contact Phone No. +001 (803) 618-2250
trkemp@PlantationQuilts.com

Teresa Kemp

Information:

Books

Teresa is in the process of setting up an on-line store, virtual Learning Portal, Programs & classes and Virtual Museum Tours as a result of the Covid-19 pandemic. She currently has 3 new books being shopped to publishers.

It has been a steep learning curve of upgrading Cell phones, computers, internet speeds and learning the streaming platforms and testing software to accomplish her goals by October 2020.

Social Media:

Google – Googled my name Teresa R. Kemp 4,420,000 results (0.46 seconds)

7278 Views of Downloads of book on PicAFile.com of Keeper of the Fire

Facebook – 2,107 friends on Facebook sites

- Teresa R. Kemp 1,601 friends
- Mrs. Teresa R. Kemp (Author Pg.) 236 friends liked this
- UGRR Quilt Code Museum – 165 friends liked this
- SC Wild's Heritage Center – 105 friend liked this

Instagram – 758 Followers

LinkedIn – 8070, Over 300 look at my LI profile daily)

- Teresa R. Kemp

Twitter – 424 Total followers

- @ugrrquiltmuseum -166 followers
- @trtkemp - 258 Followers

UGRR Quilt Museum Blog - 21,779 Total page views

- https://ugrrquiltcode.blogspot.com/2020/?m=0

Youtube.com - 4,793 views (45 subscribers)

I wanted to include some of the media coverage on the Underground Railroad Quilt Code Legacy so you can see how controversial this topic has been. I have included opinions who were neutral, some for and many who did not believe symbols were used as maps and information. Sadly, it shows that they were just uneducated on African history, art, culture who has done textiles and had symbolic textile languages for centuries before Europeans inhabited America.

I had hoped that this will be the beginning of putting some of the doubts to rest. My Book, "Keeper of the Fire an Igbo Metalsmith from Awka" ends all the controversy. It has a 500-book bibliography, 33 countries of archives libraries and museums and over 2,000 photos (according to interns) on the migration of my ancestors from East Africa to West doing textiles, hunting, weaving, agriculture, mining, and the lost wax process. They were captured in West Africa and taken to 82 countries worldwide where they continued in building and their trades enslaved and free. This book covers back to 948 BC.

It was later found that abolitionist, Freddrick Douglass's wife Anna, and her quilting group knew and used this African symbolic language we call the

UGRR Quilt Code. Their motto was, "May the points of our needles prick the hearts of slave masters."

It has also been proven that the West African Adinkra Symbols and Akan symbols (some surviving in the USA in the UGRR Quilt Code) were found in excavations in the East African pyramids in the Valley of the Kings and on rulers from the Mesopotamia River Valley (Eastern Africa) found buried by Sir Charles Thurston Shaw CBE FBA FSA to have been was an English archaeologist, the first trained specialist to work in what was then British West Africa. He specialized in the ancient cultures of present-day Ghana and Nigeria. Ibo-Ukwu in Nigeria (West Africa) was his greatest work.

Port of Harlem Magazine March 2 - March 15, 2017 Anthony (Tony)Browder

"But one of his biggest finds says Browder, was when, "I discovered a Sankofa symbol on the ceiling of two 25th dynasty tombs - - evidence proving that we traveled from the Nile to the Niger, to the Potomac and Mississippi."

He added, more specifically, that the discovery "adds weight to the oral traditions of Africans in Ghana, Mali, Senegal, Nigeria, Cameroon, Togo, and Benin who said their ancestors migrated from the Nile River Valley into the Niger River Valley centuries ago."

*(This is not an exhaustive list on our website we will keep an updated pdf.)

"Putting it in Perspective: The Symbolism of Underground Railroad Quilts" by Kris Driessen www.quilthistory.com/ugrrquilts.htm

June 24, 2007 Sunday, "Debating the Legends of Quilts as UGRR Maps" http://www.breakingnewsagency.com/english/NID_6921/

"Betsy Ross Redux: The Underground Railroad Quilt Code" by Leigh Fellner: ugrrquilt.hartcottagequilts.com

Quilt Codes and the Underground Railroad in America

"Barbara Brackman, Patricia Cummings, Leigh Fellner and Kimberly Wulfert are all quilt historians with web sites devoted to the quilt code controversy." The Unitarian and Universal Church

"Barbara Brackman, a renowned quilt historian, even published her own book called Facts & Fabrications; Unraveling the History of Quilts and Slavery (C & T Publishing) to present what she considers to be an accurate assessment of slavery, quilts and the Underground Railroad.

The International Quilt Study Center at the University of Nebraska has recorded an even-handed, 44-minute iTune lecture by Laura Horton, if you have a fast connection. (The site includes a free iTune download). Laurel Horton is a folklorist and an internationally known quilt researcher. A native of Kentucky, she earned a B.A. in English and an M.S. in Library Science from the University of Kentucky, and an M.A. degree in Folklore from the University of North Carolina - Chapel Hill.

Follow the Drinking Gourd (National Security Agency-NSA) [Ed. Note: This NSA page presents the codes as fact. It does not mention the controversy raging around the codes. The NSA evaluates information for a living, and the fate of our nation hangs on their professional ability. I do my evaluating for fun, at night, after a couple of glasses of wine. Why was I able to find the controversy and they were not?]

University of Denver - Hanson - Underground Railroad - DU Portfolio: https://portfolio.du.edu/downloadItem/96303

The Underground Railroad was neither underground nor a railroad. …. Secret Codes in Slave Quilts from the National Security Agency Central Security Service.

Slave Quilt Exhibit, another page on the NSA site, says "Most historians consider the stories involving the quilts to be more legend than fact." The NSA's left hand does not know what its right hand is doing, evidently. One wonders if there are other places where this is true.

Black Threads: Explorations in African-American Quilting, Quilt History, Fabrics, and other Fanciful Topics.
http://blackthreads.blogspot.com/

June 4, 2001 CRITIQUE: Hidden in Plain View: The Secret Story of Quilts and the Underground Railroad by Giles R. Wright

http://historiccamdencounty.com/ccnews11_doc_01a.shtml

May 6, 2004 - Flathead Valley Community College "Quilt Code Patterns"/ "Quilt Blocks & Codes":

http://searchable.opencdhost.com/look/The_Underground_Railroad_Quilt_Codes/Quilt_Blocks__Flathead_Valley_Community_College/aHRocDovL2h ybWUyLmZ2Y2MuZWR1L35jZ3JlaWcvZmluYWwvYmxvY2tzLmhobWw=_blog

2005 The Underground Railroad and the Use of Quilts as Messengers for Fleeing Slaves by Kimberly Wulfert, Ph.D.:
http://www.antiquequiltdating.com/The_Underground_Railroad_and_the_Use_of_Quilts_as_Messengers_for_Fleeing_Slaves.html

An American Quilt Myth: The Secret Quilt Code of the Underground Railroad by Patricia L. Cummings, quilt historian.

Threads of Freedom: The Underground Railroad Story in Quilts, an exhibit at Oberlin College in Oberlin, Ohio.

Daily Kos - SUN FEB 24, 2013 10:34 AM PST Underground Railroad Quilt Code by Melanie IA:

http://www.dailykos.com/blog/Melanie%20in%20IA/

Also republished by dkoma, street prophets, barriers, and bridges, dk quilt guild, and history for kossacks.

October 14, 2014 UGRR Tour in Germantown Offers 'Hidden History' Lessons: www.newsworks.org

JACQUELIN TOBIN & RAYMOND DOBARD (Co- Authors HIPV)

12/02/99 - Tobin "Unraveling the Code in Quilts" By Karen S. Peterson, USA TODAY

http://usatoday30.usatoday.com/life/enter/books/b962.htm

February 5, 2004 "Did Quilts Hold Codes to the Underground Railroad?" by Sarah Ives for National Geographic News:
http://news.nationalgeographic.com/news/2004/02/0205_040205_slaveq uilts.html

Greenway Elementary School – Quilt Debate:
http://www.beaverton.k12.or.us/greenway/leahy/ugrr/quiltsdebate.htm

February 5, 2004 "Did Quilts Hold Codes to the Underground Railroad?" by Sarah Ives for National Geographic News:
http://news.nationalgeographic.com/news/2004/02/0205_040205_slaveq uilts.html

Wikipedia Quilts of the Underground Railroad – Wikipedia

en.wikipedia.org/wiki/Quilts_of_the_Underground_Railroad

Jun 4, 2001 - Critique of Book, Hidden in Plain View:

historiccamdencounty.com/ccnews11_doe_01a.shtml Aside from the oral testimony of Ozella McDaniel Williams, the book offers no documentation for its thesis, relying instead on sheer conjecture...

Apr 3, 2006 - Barbara Brackman - Fact Sheet on the "Quilt Code": www.antiquequiltdating.com/Fact_Sheet_on_the_Quilt_Code.html

... A journalist and teacher, who said she first heard about the codes when she bought a quilt from a woman named Ozella McDaniel Williams at...

April 3, 2007 Time Magazine "Unravelling the Myth of Quilts and the Underground" Dobard's interpretations of the geometric configurations of certain quilt blocks is based on the oral statements of Ozella McDaniel Williams, a quilt vendor in...

http://content.time.com/time/arts/article/0,8599,1606271,00.html
content.time.com/time/arts/article/0,8599,1606271,00.html

Feb 16, 2008 - The source of this information was Ozella McDaniel Williams, a descendant of slaves who made and sold quilts in South Carolina. She was...

Feb 18, 2008 - Black History How Freedom Quilts were used as Signals Maps By: Katrina Murphy:

http://www.humanities360.com/index.php/black-history-how-freedom-quilts-were-used-as-signals-maps-underground-5-58249/

October 28, 2010 National Geographic. Did Quilts Hold the Codes to the UGRR?

http://news.nationalgeographic.com/news/2004/02/0205_040205_slaveq uilts_2.html

Jan 1, 2011 The Underground Railroad story in quilts - The Mennonite www.themennonite.org/.../The_Underground_Railroad_story_in_quilts

- Retired educator and quilter Ozella McDaniel Williams from Charleston, SC, shared

the secret codes embedded in quilts to assist runaway...

SERENA STROTHER WILSON

Nov. 1999 Call and Post "Slave Escape Codes Were Hidden in Quilts" Photos by Tobais Houpe

Jan. 2000 The Columbus Dispatch Columbus, OH "Slave Escape Codes Were Hidden in Quilts"

Jan. 2000 The Columbus Dispatch Columbus, OH "Black History Month - Storyteller Weaves History with Quilts Powerful Messages" by Robert Albrecht dispatch Staff Reporter

Feb. 2002 Williamson Daily News Williamson, WV Quilt Program Planned by Williamson Branch NAACP & Youth Council

The UGRR Quilt Code has not been well received by all. The following excerpts were all publicly placed on-line and are here since they are part of the coverage of the UGRR Quilt Code and our family History.

Feb. 2002 Williamson Daily News Williamson, WV "Speaker Looks Back on History" by Audrey Carter News Editor Dr. Howard & Serena Wilson Sponsor NAACP

Mar. 29, 2002 11:42:54 EST Quilt History

From: Palampore@aol.com To:

Traditional Quiltworks (issue 79, until May 13, 2002) has an article out right now which tells of a woman who says her great-grandmother taught her family this secret code. They have an article---EXCLUSIVE Underground Railroad Quilts: More Secrets Revealed---This is a headline on the cover.

My parents always said they know people who do not believe in the African Holocaust, the Jewish Holocausts that anyone ever went to the moon and Jesus Christ. We just present the truth as we know it. I am presenting the case of millions enslaved in Human Trafficking today! Teresa R. Kemp

Inside the Inside the story is: THE SECRET QUILT CODE by Serena Strother Wilson. She is a niece of the woman in SC who told Tobin this story. Apparently, the family is now fighting for the old aunt's story to be kept alive. This woman has a section in the back that says that she and her husband are available to give speeches, and they have a museum exhibit. She says this secret was never shared outside of her family until her aunt told it in SC at the market.

You must see some these patterns she claims were used. One is the sun bonnet southern belle of the 1940's and she writes, "In the northern states, Free Black and white women wore long dresses with Sue Bonnets. In the Quilt Code, the Sue Bonnet and Bandanna helped women recognize the clothes they would be given to wear in the Northern States." This is 1 of 19 patterns she gives and then writes how it fits into the "Secret Code".

I am not writing this to be mean, I am saying that this is unfair for history to be rewritten in this manner with no true documentation to back it up. I have a quilt which has a tag on it that says that it belonged to Wealthy Stoddard. She died in 1861. The newspaper inside the quilt is dated Jan. 20, 1869. I immediately knew that the person who wrote the tag found this quilt in Wealthy's belongings and made an assumption, that it belonged to her. But it did not, it belonged to a family member of her's who was alive after Jan. 20, 1869. I can no longer say it is a quilt which belonged to Wealthy Stoddard. It belonged to someone in her family. Thanks for listening. Lynn Gorges

http://www.quilthistory.com/2002/082.htm

8/19/2003 Underground Railroad Station - In addition to honoring the women autoworkers and showcasing Michigan's automobile heritage, the museum will also highlight the role of the Wayne County men and women who helped blacks escaping slavery during the Civil War. It will house items gathered from former workers and their families, and the Plymouth Historical Museum will lend some of its collection. A Belleville quilt-maker will assist with the Underground Railroad aspect. Secret codes were embedded in quilts and quilted pillowcases to instruct escapees in their movements north. Noted African-American author Serena Strother Wilson will aid in preparing the exhibits.

Source: Wayne County Department of Public Services, Division of Parks. www.UAW.org

http://heelspurs.com/cgi-bin/_search.cgi?a=yes&keyword=serena&n=y

2004 In book: Quilting to Soothe the Soul: Create Memories for Today, Tomorrow & Forever by Linda Giesler Carlton

August 23, 2004, 11:15 AM "CBS Commemorating Slaves Freedom": http://www.cbsnews.com/news/commemorating-slaves-freedom/

August 24, 2004 "So what do you think?" http://www.peta-ucks.com/smf/index.php?topic=1640.0

Sept. 17, 2004 UNESCO 10th Year of the Family Celebration Worldwide Women's Organization

Salt Lake Community College at the Miller Campus 9750 South 300 West, Sandy, Utah

Program Book

http://scrivovivo.typepad.com/bookofdays/files/womens-voice-final.pdf

September 20th, 2004 The Digital University Newspaper Brigham Young University, Provo, Utah

http://universe.byu.edu/2004/09/20/underground-railroad-story-retold-by-posterity/

History Makers: 3/16/2005 History Makers - Art Maker & Education Maker

http://www.thehistorymakers.com/biography/serena-strother-wilson-40

Videos of Serena Strother Wilson by the History Makers 31 Stories (See Ordered Story Set)

http://www.idvl.org/thehistorymakers/Bio306.html

Our research continued after these interviews and now we know Milton was listed as Mulattoe in the US Census 1880 (White planter father David Richardson Strother & Native American mother, Ann Jones – Eastern Cherokee & Choctaw) We found a Strother sibling who they never knew Dave and an infant Strother child's death record bring the total of children of Milton Strother to 17. Link to the History Makers Tapes Go to the Library of Congress - News Articles:

Articles:
http://www.usatoday.com/story/news/nation/2014/06/24/library-of-congress-history-makers/11339613/
http://www.nytimes.com/2014/06/24/us/library-of-congress-to-host-collection-of-african-american-interviews.html
http://www.wsfa.com/story/25963748/african-american-archive-history-makers-moves-to-library-of-congress
http://diverseeducation.com/article/65484/

www.idvl.org/thehistorymakers/Bio306.htm 31 Stories (See Ordered Story Set)

Slating of Serena Wilson interview

Serena Wilson shows a Nigerian sankofa bird carving and explains its meaning

Serena Wilson's favorites

Serena Wilson describes her mother's background and ancestors

Serena Wilson describes her father, a white man who married across the color line and supported black rights

Serena Wilson discusses Reconstruction in Edgefield County, South Carolina, and her interracial ancestry

Serena Wilson talks about her father's lessons and the importance of children having pride

Serena Wilson discusses Strom Thurmond's interracial relationship

Serena Wilson shares memories of childhood in a biracial family in Edgefield, South Carolina

Serena Williams recalls her maternal grandparents and farm life

Serena Wilson remembers her grandmother's quilts and superstitions

Serena Wilson discusses her siblings and cousins

Serena Wilson recalls helping her grandmother with textile crafts

Serena Wilson describes her childhood environs, South Carolina

Serena Wilson recalls her family's quilting and other customs

Serena Wilson gives an overview of her school life

Serena Wilson talks about her children and their families

Serena Wilson discusses gender roles throughout her family's history

Serena Wilson recalls trying to avoid taking French in high school

Serena Wilson recalls her courtship and marriage at West Virginia State

Serena Wilson remembers visiting family who moved to Ohio for work

Serena Wilson recalls moving to Columbus when her husband went to Vietnam

Serena Wilson details her first teaching work in Columbus, Ohio, 1968

Serena Wilson recalls trips to Paris while her husband was stationed in Germany on Valentine's Day every year

Serena Wilson describes her renewed interest in quilting

Serena Wilson discusses her quilt shops and making quilts for family

Serena Wilson recalls her family's superstitions and psychic powers

Serena Wilson discusses African symbols in quilt patterns, the "quilt code" and the popularity of black culture

Serena Wilson shares final reflections

Serena Wilson considers her legacy

Serena Wilson discusses the recording of African-American history April 3, 2007 Time Entertainment "Unravelling the Myth of Quilts and the Railroad" http://content.time.com/time/arts/article/0,8599,1606271,00.html#ixzz1kFHr6RV9

June 7, 2011 Tuesday, The Valley Voice: Stitched into Freedom: The Role of Quilts in the Underground Railroad by Cookie Steponaitis: http://www.vvoice.org/?module=displaystory&story_id=2329&format=html&edition_id=283

Nov. 11, 2011 Gordon-Lee Mansion event evokes 'Gone with the Wind'

http://www.timesfreepress.com/news/2011/nov/11/have-a-ball/

Feb. 2012 Serena Wilson Obituary:

http://www.legacy.com/obituaries/dispatch/obituary.aspx?pid=155868803

February 18, 2013 Southern West Virginia Community and Technical College
http://www.southernwv.edu/?q=node/12390

July 2014 Serena Wilson's Tapes are in the Library of Congress

http://www.linkedin.com/groups?newItemsAbbr=&gid=8108867&trk=groups_guest_most_popular-h-srp

June 2013 Former WVSU national alumni association president dies www.wvgazette.com/News/201306050198 June 6, 2013 Former WVSU Alumni Dies http://www.highbeam.com/doc/1P2-34739313.html Jun 5, 2013 West Virginia Sentinel Howard Wilson Dies www.westvirginiasentinal.com/tag/teresa-wilson-kemp/ 2013 WVSU Annual Report: http://www.wvstateu.edu/getattachment/Alumni/West-Virginia-State-Foundation/WVSU-Foundation/Foundation-Annual-Report.pdf.aspx

Jun 6, 2013 - Howard Wilson, a veteran and former president of West Virginia State University's National Alumni Association, has died.

City of Columbus - File #: 0158X-2013 https://columbus.legistar.com/LegislationDetail.aspx?ID...

OPHELIA DEVORE MITCHELL

Link to Ophelia's interview: http://www.thehistorymakers.com/bi

ography/ophelia-devore-41
www.OpheliaDevore.com
en.wikipedia.org/wiki/Ophelia_DeVore

http://thegrio.com/2013/05/09/ophelia-devore-founder-of-first-black-model-agency-teams-up-with-emory-university/
www.dogwoodandpalmetto.com/carolina-girls-ophelia-devore-mitchell/

http://www.timesfreepress.com/news/2013/may/21/empowering-black-women-ophelia-devore-shrewd-georg/

http://www.ledger-enquirer.com/2014/03/02/2981574/ophelia-devore-mitchell-dies-at.html

http://www.aaregistry.org/historic_events/view/ophelia-devore-held-savvy-attractiveness

http://www.nytimes.com/2014/03/13/nyregion/ophelia-devore-mitchell-91-dies-redefined-beauty.html?_r=0

https://www.facebook.com/joy.hinton.50/posts/10203050378643440

http://newsone.com/2945473/ophelia-devore-dies-dead/

http://news.emory.edu/stories/2013/05/upress_ophelia_deVore_papers/campus.html

http://www.visionaryproject.org/devoremitchellophelia/

http://www.washingtonpost.com/national/ophelia-devore-mitchell-pioneering-modeling-agent-dies-at-92/2014/03/16/801cd924-ab89-11e3-98f6-8e3c562f9996_story.html

http://www.timesfreepress.com/news/2013/may/21/empowering-black-women-ophelia-devore-shrewd-georg/

http://www.ebony.com/style/ophelia-devore-bold-beauty-and-brains#axzz3GwMPt4Cd

http://www.poemhunter.com/ophelia-devore-mitchell/biography/

http://madamenoire.com/278097/emory-university-acquires-papers-of-fashion-and-business-trailblazer-ophelia-devore/

OPHELIA IN VIDEOS

http://www.youtube.com/watch?v=m3a-TI6cEpc

http://www.youtube.com/watch?v=Q91FtJoIAtM

Ophelia DeVore Model Citizen
http://madamenoire.com/278097/emory-university-acquires-papers-of-fashion-and-business-trailblazer-ophelia-devore/

TERESA R. KEMP

Nana Efua Adadzewa 1st

May 25th, 2020 Facebook Live: ONE AFRICA-USA DAY "Unveiling Slavery Together" Program Teresa Kemp at 10:30 AM EST (7:30 am PT) for a Panel Discussion on Trans-Atlantic Slavery United Nations/UNESCO Day of Remembrance.

9:00 PST/11:00 am EST Teresa R. Kemp Presents:

Slave Names Database, Trans-Atlantic Slave Voyages,

https://www.youtube.com/watch?v=-gtFq9URQDo

CA Slave Insurance Database & Native American and White Slavery in America.

CA Slave Era Insurance Registry Overview by Teresa R. Kemp vimeo.com › Videos May 21, 2020 - Ms. Teresa R. Kemp Presents this infomercial for her Free On-Line Presentation May 25th, 2020 at 9:15 am Pacific Time (PT)

March 19th, 2020 Promoted to the rank of YonDan 4th Degree Black Belt in Matsubayashi Shorin-Ryu Okinawan Karate Do Rick Moore Academy, Columbus Ohio by Hanshi Rick Moore my instructor of 45 years. (I retired 34 years ago and last year started training as a result of heart issues.)

January 4, 2020 Took 3 1st place awards in NASKA Karate Tournament in Joplin Missouri.

December 2019 – Finished the year #1 in UPMAC Women's 18+ Black Belt Divisions of Weapon's Kata & 2 in Kumite.

August 11, 2018 Interview by African American Literature Book Club AALBC.com Intercontinental Hotel Atlanta, GA with Troy Johnson
https://www.youtube.com/watch?v=PV0FuaJGZlc

Teresa R. Kemp Describes Her Book, Keeper of the Fire: An Igbo Metalsmith From Awka. Kemps explains that Few Americans read multi-lingual sources preserved centuries by international slavers. She also explains the quilt patterns. Using common sense as binding, primary sources the stitching, gathering African metallurgy & symbols Mrs. Kemp exposes distortions/omissions. Learn more:

https://aalbc.com/authors/author.php?author_name=Teresa+Kemp

November 18, 2017 -Teresa Kemp, Director of SC Wild's Heritage Center is at Pioneer Day in Lincolnton, Georgia at Lincoln County Historical Park's Original Quilting House! https://www.wctel.net/events/teresa-r-kemp-ugrr-quilts-at-pioneer-day/

March 24, 2017 WJBF Augusta GA's Channel 6 News Reported by: Samantha Williams

https://www.wjbf.com/news/mccormick-county-programs-help-at-risk-youth/

Jan 16, 2017: Jan 16, 2017 by McCormick, SC's Teresa R. Kemp talks about secret quilt codes for the www.indexjournal.com › news › mccormick-scs-teresa-r-Kemp...

McCormick, SC's **Teresa R. Kemp** talks about secret quilt codes.

SATURDAY, 22 AUGUST 2015 Teresa R Kemp, African American historian, traces her origin to Oka, Igboland

http://re-thinkingafrica.blogspot.com/2015/08/by-biafra-diboh-slightly-editedfrom.html

January 1, 2015 Bernice Bennett's Program, "Research at the National Archives and Beyond",

Discussion of book "Keeper of the Fire" with Teresa R. Kemp by Bernice Bennett
www.blogtalkradio.com ›2015/01/16

American Civil War Story's Mark Weaver Interviewed Ms. Teresa R. Kemp, Military Historian. Visit his site:

http://www.americancivilwarstory.com/underground-railroad-interview.html

– Sept. 21st, 2014 Gist of Freedom Radio Interview "African Facial Marks Decode UGRR Quilts"

http://www.blogtalkradio.com/thegistoffreedom/2014/09/22/africans-facial-marks-decode-underground-railroad-quilts-w-teresa-kemp

Sept. 5-17th, 2014 "UGRR Secrets of the Quilts & Stop Human Trafficking" at Tennessee Temple University in Chattanooga, TN

August 2014 Mrs. Teresa R. Kemp - Underground Railroad Interview Part 1 & Part 2 - American Civil War Stories: www.americancivilwarstory.com/underground-railroad-interview.html

July 1 - Aug. 1st, 2014 July Dawn Art Show at the Atlanta AFPLS Teresa R. Kemp Exhibitor

July 24-27th, 2014 The 1st World Igbo Arts & Cultural Festival at Frontier Museum in Staunton, VA Paper & Presentation - "UGRR Secrets of the Quilts & Stop Human Trafficking"

May 10th, 2014 "Sampler Show" Ephesus Liturgical Art Show Ephesus Seven Day Adventist Church in Columbus, Ohio

April 9th, 2014 "1800's in Family Plantation Quilts" Quilters for Christ Quilt Guild in Columbus, Ohio

March 26-28th, 2014 Mancuso Quilt Fest Destination Savannah UGRR Secrets of the Quilts & Stop Human Trafficking at Intl. Trade & Convention Center Savannah, GA

March 1, 2014 Kaiser Permanente KPAAPA Community Health Fair "UGRR Secrets of the Quilts & Stopping Human Trafficking" in Decatur, GA

Feb. 28th, 2014 UGRR Secrets of the Quilts & Stopping Human Trafficking (Dr. & Nurses) at Kaiser Permanente Regional Headquarters Atlanta GA

Feb 16th, 2014 "UGRR Secrets of the Quilts & Stop Human Trafficking" - Youth Black History Program at Mt. Zion AME Church Lone Star, SC

Feb. 15th, 2014 "UGRR Secrets of the Quilts & Stop Human Trafficking" The

Cornbread Jubilee & Festival of Breads in Columbia South Carolina

Feb. 5th-8th, 2014 at Covina Library Covina CA UGRR Secrets of the Quilt Exhibit & Stop Human Trafficking

March 14th - April 27th, 2013 "Memories Pieced Together" at MLK Arts Complex Columbus Ohio

March 22-24th, 2013 - World Igbo Assembly Staunton, VA

March 30-31st, 2013 "Women Empowered to Achieve the Impossible" Baltimore, MD

Feb. 20th, 2013 "Track your Freedom Program" at Washington Pk Branch/Annie Mc Pheeters 1116 MLK Jr., Dr. Atlanta, GA 30314

Feb. 15-17th, 2013 365° Harmony Honoring Serena Wilson in Williamson, WV by Teresa Kemp & Dr. Howard Wilson

Oct. 8, 2012 Atlanta Black Star 'Quilt Codes' Helped Slaves Navigate the Underground Railroad to Freedom | Posted by Stan Jun 26, 2013 - Title: To honor, recognize and celebrate the long and fulfilling life of Dr. Howard L. Wilson and extend our sincerest condolences to his family …

Oct. 5, 2012 Traveling quilts on display at W.Va. State chedit.sx4.de.publicus.com/News/201210050037

Oct 5, 2012 - Teresa R. Kemp is traveling the country to share centuries of her family's … members are WVSU alumni — including her father, Howard Wilson

Oct. 8, 2012 Quilt codes Helped Slaves Navigate the UGRR to Freedom.

http://atlantablackstar.com/2012/10/08/quilt-codes-helped-slaves-navigate-the-underground-railroad-to-freedom/

Oct. 1, 2012 "Quilt Exhibit at WVSU Depicts Slaves' Journey Along Underground Railroad"

Historic exhibit part of W.Va. State University Homecoming Week http://www.wvstateu.edu/announcement/2012/10/01/Quilt-Exhibit-at-WVSU-Depicts-Slaves%E2%80%99-Journey-Alon.aspx

Boy's group at the UGRR Secret Quilt Code Museum Exhibit learning about the different wood types, the needed skills, and techniques of the master Nigerian Wood Carvers.

Oct. 2012 "The Stinger" WVSU Institute, WV

Oct. 2012 The Charleston Gazette Charleston, WV Oct. 15, 2012 Atlanta Cyclorama –

www.anogusa.org/Guest_book.htm
www2.atlanta.net/.../eventSearch.aspx
www.ocaatlanta.com/.../Atlanta%20OCA%20Annual%20Report%2021

Nov. 2010 Concord Press, Athens, WV

Nov. 17, 2010 Applied for NTF http://www.nps.gov/subjects/ugrr/ntf_member/ntf_partner_results.htm

Oct. 2010 UGRR Secret Quilt Messages Program Presented at Bluefield State College "UGRR Messages in Quilts & Songs Sponsored by Title III 2006 - Quilt Code Museum Commercial "Shhh"
www.youtube.com/watch?v=2uNHREQheqs

Quilt Code Museum in Underground Atlanta Georgia www.gpb.org/stateofthearts/term/quilt Georgia Public Broadcasting - The code has been passed on to Ozella's niece, Serena Wilson, and Wilson's daughter, Teresa R. Kemp, who is director of the Underground Railroad Quilt

May 2004 Salt Lake City Tribune" Road Maps to History" Salt Lake City, Utah by Rhina Guidos Photo by Steve Griffin Salt Lake City Tribune Staff

Nov. 1999 National Geographic "Hidden Messages in Quilt Designs" by Raymond Dobard Art by Jennifer Christiansen, NGS Staff

Oct. 1999 The Daily News Williamson, WV. Reported on "Quilts gave more than warmth to slaves on the UGRR in the 1800's" by Serena Wilson & Viola Witcher, her sister.

Ambassador Bope's tapes in the museum for "Brotherhood Against Apartheid" UGRR Secret Quilt Code Museum's Director, Mrs. Teresa R. Kemp discusses the impact of instruction on the African males image, on her son in Atlanta, GA Public Schools Systems.

Teresa R. Kemp, teaching 5-8 yr. old boys to sew at St. Phillips Church summer camp.

# CONTACT US –

I would love to hear your questions, comments, and opinions.

Phone: Outside the USA by phone: +001 (404) 468-7050

On-Line:
- Blog: http://UGRRQuiltCode.BlogSpot.com
- Email: trkemp@PlantationQuilts.com/trkemp@hotmail.com

Facebook Book Pages:
- Mrs. Teresa R. Kemp
- SC Wild's Heritage Center
- UGRR Secret Quilt Code Museum

LinkedIn:
- Mrs. Teresa R. Kemp

Twitter:
- @UGRRQuiltMuseum
- @trtkemp

Website:
- www.PlantationQuilts.com

Youtube.com
- Teresa R. Kemp Keeper of the Fire Playlist

Phone: Outside the USA by phone:

(Country Code) +001 (404) 468-7050

We have created unique programs for:
- ☐ Business/Governments/Professional Associations
- ☐ Social Clubs/Churches/At-Risk Populations
- ☐ Corporate "Lunch and Learns"/Team Building/ Diversity
- ☐ Libraries/Museums/Archives/Conference Centers
- ☐ Fraternities/Sororities/School and Family Reunions
- ☐ Colleges/Universities/Schools and Home School Associations K-12
- ☐ Grade appropriate state requirements, hands on and interactive/ Research Centers
- ☐ Community Centers/Camps/After-School Programs/ Home School Scholars
- ☐ Medical Associations/Health Fairs/ Community Programs/Book Clubs
- ☐ Rites of Passage/Juneteenth Celebrations/Festivals/State Fairs

"We Have Chosen Education as a Bridge to Understanding"

Contact us for speaking engagements & exhibits that heal communities!

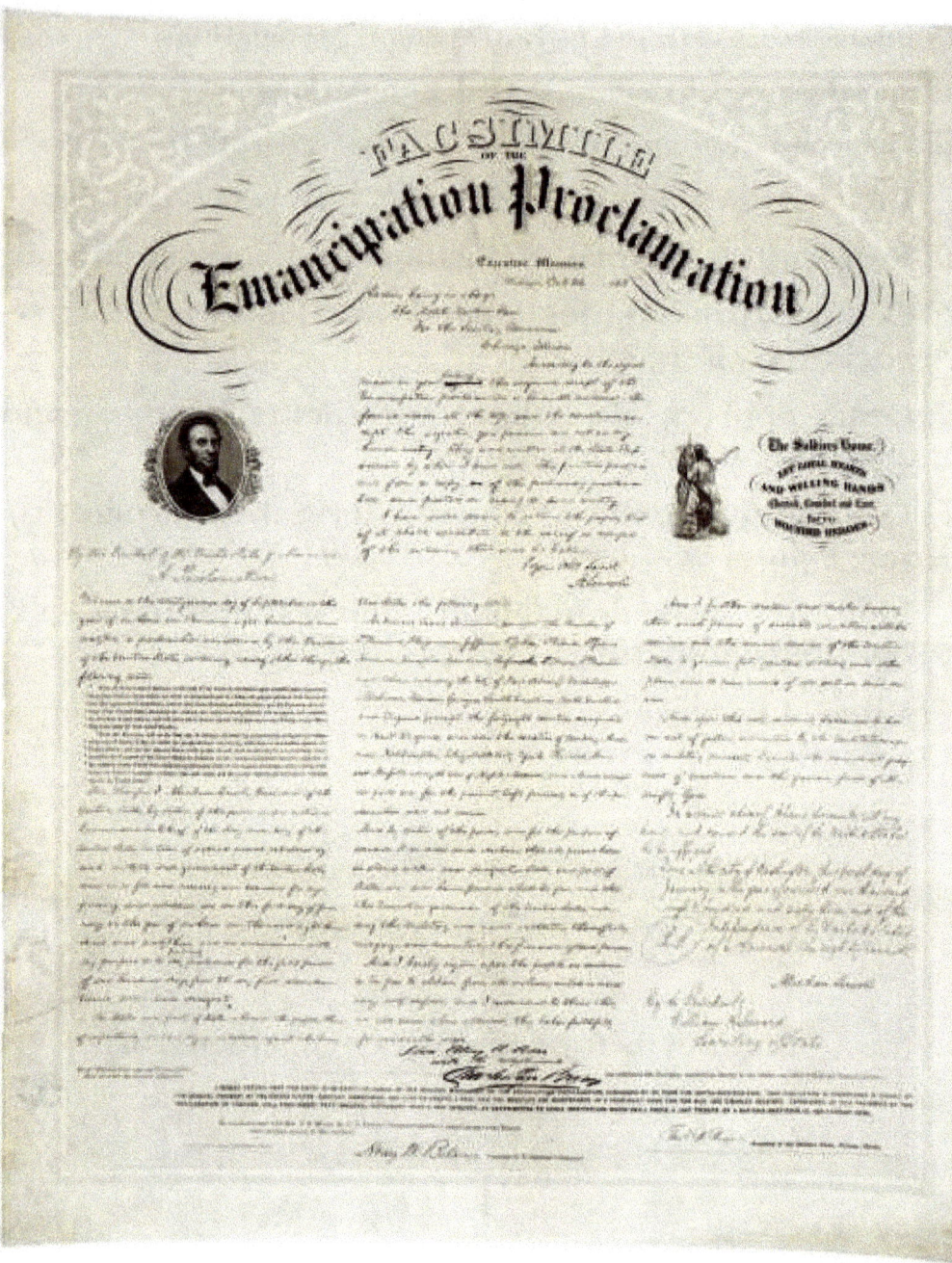

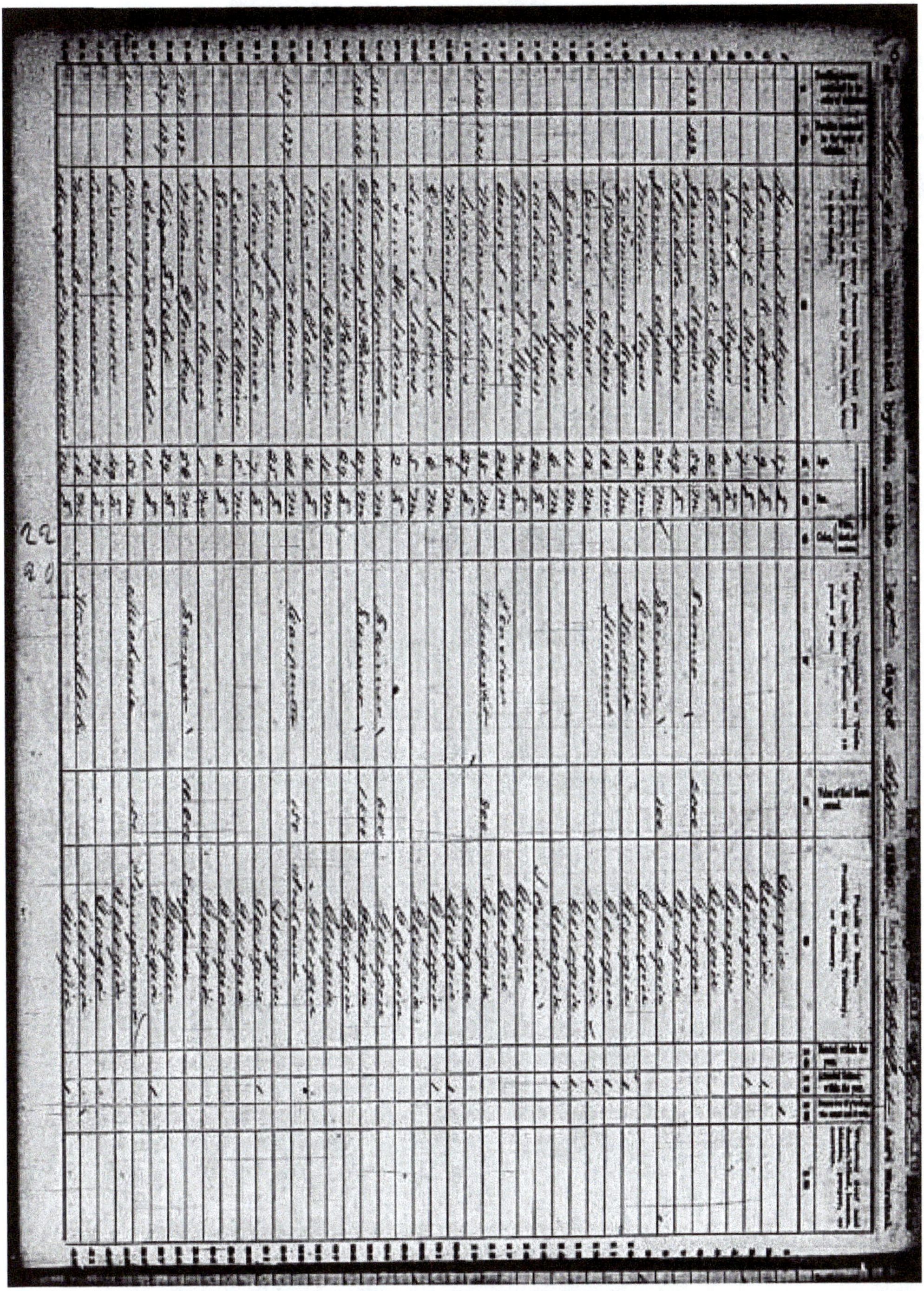

FACES OF RAP MOTHERS – BOOK FOUR

Faces of Rap Mothers Enterprise
DonnaInk Publications | Beat Deep Books
www.donnainkpublications.com | www.facesofrapmothers.com

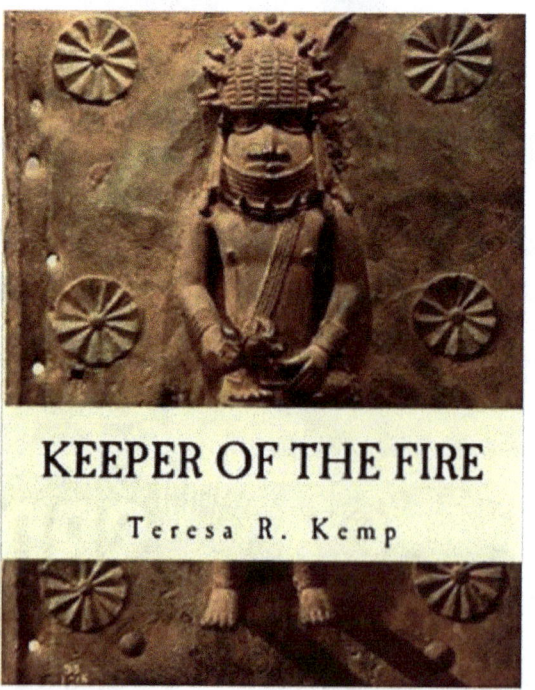

CHAPTER ELEVEN

NAKENDRA HARRIS-MASON

CANDY STROTHER DEVORE MITCHELL

NAKENDRA HARRIS-MASON IS A 34-YEAR-OLD author from Los Angeles Ca, who has spent most of her time residing in San Bernardino County. Nakendra is also a wife and mother of four sons and two stepsons. Nakendra has written and published two books, titled: *Who Am I* and *Marriage Made & What Comes Within*. She is working on her third title, *I Found Me*.

As an independent television reality show film creator as executive producer and director alongside her husband, Marvin Mason, Nakendra's show called, Marriage Made airs on the MJOwn Network and several other platforms on ROKU. Nakendra's husband is her executive producer as well.

Having been in the film-industry for quite a while, more behind the scenes, Nakendra has appeared on several red carpets, such as the Oscars, Gospel Goes to Hollywood, and many private events. She has attended a handful of galas and sponsored charity events in Hollywood held by a group of her CEO boss friends she lovingly refers to them as.

Beginning the pursuit of writing in 2000, Nakendra has also written poetry, branched off to music / lyrics and wrote her first studio track with Calvin Broadus better known as Snoop Dogg in 2002. Snoop never released the song, which was understandable as Nakendra did not disclose her age until after the recording and she sixteen at the time – though mature for her age. That did not stop her from living a dream of becoming a writer.

Nakendra aids her community by feeding less unfortunate, keeping youth encouraged, and uplifting them to stay on the right track under her nonprofit organization, *You're Created To Inspire Ministries*. Most of her time currently, is spent with her family enjoying life as her own boss where she can create innovative ideas and share them with the world through books, speaking engagements, and television reality programming. Her purpose is to inspire as many people as she can who have the same drive as she does. She wants to aid those who want more and are willing to do more in life. Nakendra's plan is not only to provide people with hope, but to also be the hope people love to see. She encourages others to keep their faith and to keep going until they the results they want are achieved!

Nakendra has faced many challenges in her life and overcame each obstacle she is encountered. She has engaged audience who see her for who she is, which is authentic, truthful, funny, energetic, original, and real. As an inspiring, outgoing, and caring individual, she loves to see others win. She has not only faced challenges, but also won more battles than she has lost. Between her prayer life and personal relationship with God, Nakendra has persevered through it all. Not being the type to entice animosity or conflict, she stands for what's right and disregards negativity. She has faced her giants, some big – others small and known she has what it takes to prevail. With a seriousness regarding family, finances, and friends – Nakendra is loyal and holds high standards regarding same – believing true loyalty is hard to find in relationships, friendships, and workmanship, which others appreciate about her. Nakendra has learned to find the good in everything because it outweighs the bad. She has discovered a new level of faith that requires an enhanced version of herself. She has also decided not to allow others to make her change the way she is to fit in; if it is not original, she is not focused on it.

With a love for networking with people, Nakendra sees life and success on another level beyond poverty and comfort zones. She knows poverty and comfort zones are obstacles to success. Instead, she inspires others to reach higher until arriving at a place where an individual wants to be in life. Not focused on money, Nakendra's focus is more toward God. She believes He knows the things she requires to stay afloat and that whatever she needs God will provide. When people meet Nakendra they are impressed by her early-life wisdom and knowledge and are amazed at how she makes things happen and gets things done.

With unique style, as an outside the box woman, to meet Nakendra is to love her. She has a lot of joy from inside of her spirit that is contagious; people cling to her like a magnet, but she draws a line as she respects boundaries, believing without boundaries people easily cross one another. Keeping her faith, she stays prayed up and knowing God's plan is bigger than hers and His will her life speaks for itself. She believes God's plans are much better than plans she sets out herself. She is not afraid of fear and most importantly, she is not afraid of change or challenges because they make her grow. To that end, Nakendra Harris-Mason believes in her ability to be and do anything she puts her mind to.

CANDY STROTHER DEVORE MITCHELL

FACES OF RAP MOTHERS – BOOK FOUR

CANDY STROTHER DEVORE MITCHELL

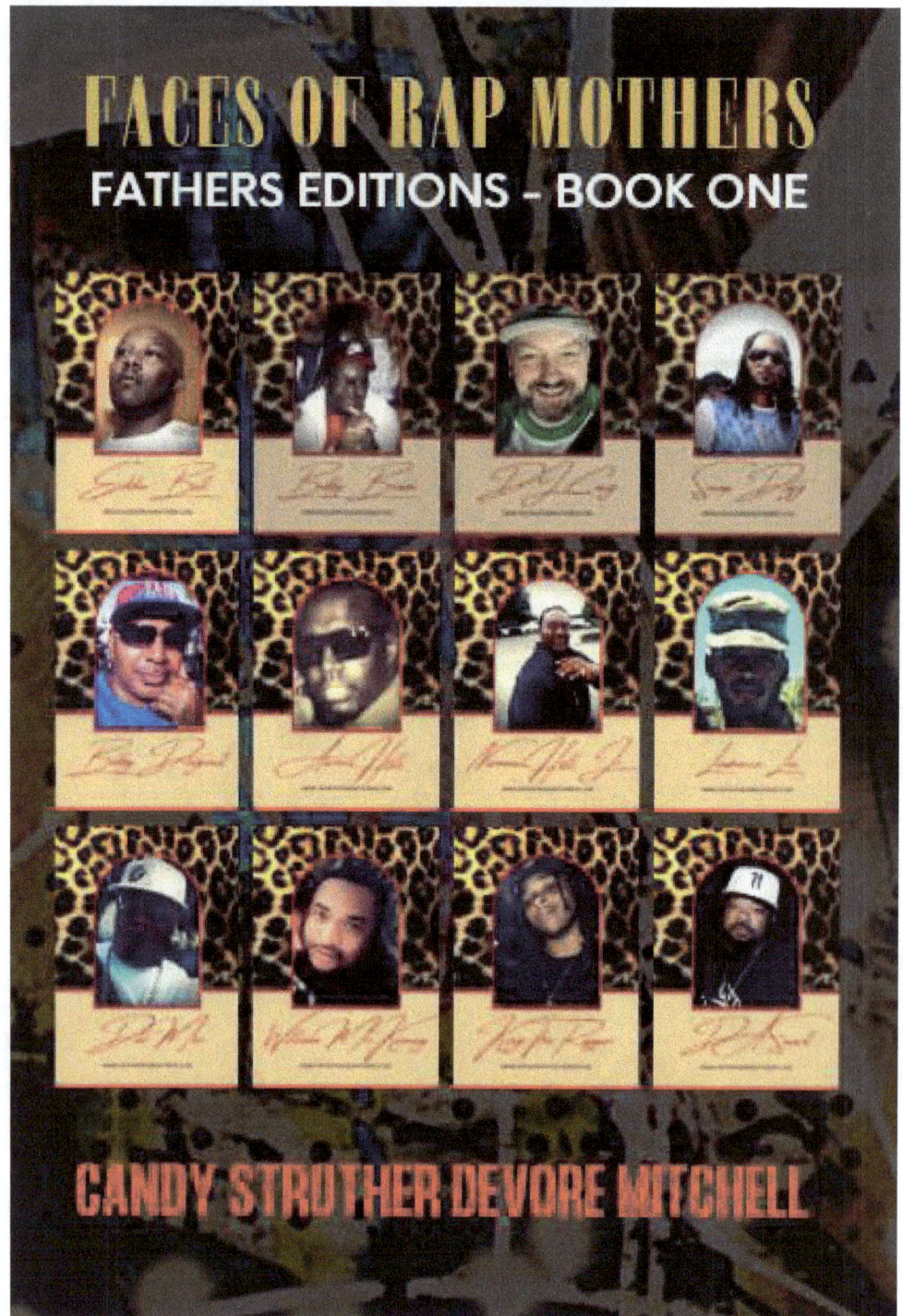

CHAPTER TWELVE

LENA MOSS

CANDY STROTHER DEVORE MITCHELL

LENA MOSS, AN ORIGINAL *Faces of Rap Mothers Member*, aka Aunt Rose baby girl is the lady of Aaron Hall – Grammy Winner and the mother of my beautiful baby cousin Kaloni Hall. Ya'll know my cousin, the beautiful Lena Moss from Book One in this series. A distant cousin to Bonnie Williams, wife of author Stanley "Tookie" Williams and niece of Dr. Ophelia DeVore-Mitchell - Civil Rights Hero who worked along with Dr Martin Luther King for civil rights makes Ms. Lena Moss a character comprised of many talents.

This is an update on Lena. When you read *Faces of Rap Mothers Book One*, you learn Lena is a hard worker. She has worked for the mayor of the largest city in the world, the Big Apple, New York City. She has also been continuously working hard to save lives during Code Blue emergencies as an essential healthcare worker during COVID. As her cousin, I am enormously proud of Lena and want to share my congratulations on her well-deserved promotion. Heavenly Father, and her job, has blessed her by showing appreciation for all her hard work and labor through a commemorative award.

Lena Moss, and her beautiful daughter Kaloni, are currently streaming live on *Faces of Rap Mothers Television Network,* which is available on ROKU using Amazon Firestick, Apple TV on PPV. Our programs also air on Muuzictyme alongside superstars Beyonce, Jennifer Lopez, and Bruno Mars through *Faces of Rap Mothers Music* video shows produced by none other than, Candy Strother DeVore-Mitchell – author of multi-book series and owner of *Faces of Rap Mothers Enterprise.*

Lena Moss and her lovely daughter are also starring on the second largest black owned network. The Now Network, broadcast since 1962 in America, Africa, and the United Kingdom through satellite television with worldwide reach.

Enjoy this updated pictorial about Lena Moss and her family.

FACES OF RAP MOTHERS – BOOK FOUR

Lena Moss as a baby.

Lena Moss & Kaloni Hall.

Lena Moss & Kaloni Hall.

& Kaloni Hall.

Lena Moss on her birthday, which is also Halloween!

Lena Moss & Aaron Hall.

Four of Lena Moss's twelve siblings from left to right: Mary Jones, Veronica Moss, Clarence DeVore, and Darryl DeVore with Lena in front.

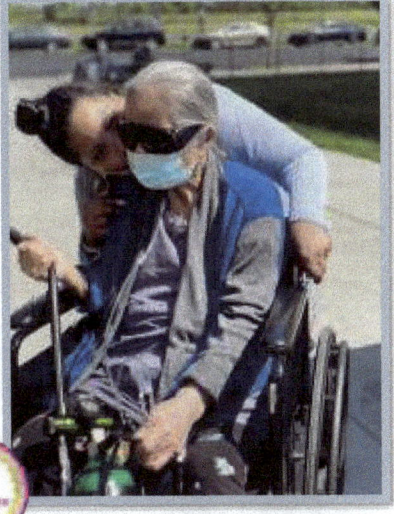

FACES OF RAP MOTHERS – BOOK FOUR

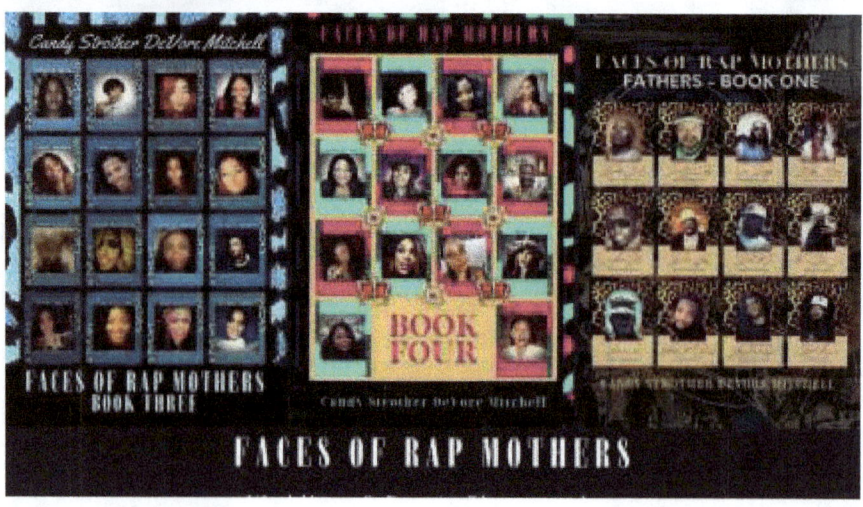

CHAPTER THIRTEEN

SUGA T

TENINA STEVENS, BETTER KNOWN BY HER stage name SUGA-**T**, is an American rapper and actress from Vallejo, California. She is a founding member of *The Click*, a rap group that includes her brothers *E-40* and *D-Shot* and her cousin *B-Legit*.

The Click released their debut album, *Down and Dirty*, in 1992 through *E-40's Sick Wid It Records*, after which all four-member released solo projects, with Suga-T's debut album *It's All Good* being released in 1993. In 1995, *Sick Wid It* signed a major label distribution deal with *Jive Records*. Suga-T then appeared on *The Click's* second album, *Game Related* in 1995, and released her major label debut, *Paper Chasin'*, which charted on the *Billboard* 200 at No. 193.

Suga-T sings multi-genre music, writes songs, and is a television and music executive producer. Currently working as an author, performer, speaker, and vision partner coach, Suga-T is the founder of *Sprinkle Me Enterprise* and *Sprinkle Me School of Music and Vision*. At one time she sacrificed her career to return to school to complete her Associate of Arts in business, her Bachelor of Arts in psychology and her Master's in organizational management. Suga-T re-invented her brand and aids others in reinventing their brands.

- *All Good* – Sick Wid It - 1993

- *Paper Chase* – Sick Wid It – 1996

- *Be About It* – Sprinkle Me Enterprise – 2007

- *The Game Needs Me* – Sprinkle Me Enterprise / Inspirationz by Suga, Inc. - 2010

Collaboration Albums
- *Down and Dirty* - The Click - 1992
- *Game Related* - The Click - 1995
- *Money & Muscle* - The Click - 2001

Compilation Albums
- *Gettin' It* - 2000

Mixtapes
- *The Return of Suga-T: The Best Is Yet to Come* - 2010

Extended Plays
- *The All Woman Show* - 2011
- *Queen of the West* - 2017

Soundtrack Appearances
- *Hot Ones Echo Thru the Ghetto* - 1995
- *On the Grind* - 1996
- *Gotta Have Game* - 1996
- *Why You Wanna Funk* - 1996
- *Struggled & Survived* - 1997
- *If You Don't Want None* - 2000
- *Who Owns It* - 2000
- *Comin' Up on Somp'n* - 2001
- *Captain Save a Hoe* - 2013

Filmography[edit]

Film[edit]

- *Obstacles* - 2000
- *Malibooty* - 2003
- *Born to Be a Gangster* - 2003
- *What Are the Chances* - 2016
- *16 Bars* - 2017

Television[edit]

- *The Lyricist Lounge Show* - 2000
- Unsung - Season 9 Episode 4 - 2016
- *Hip Hop Honors: All Hail the Queens* – 2016
- *Young Grandmothers of Hip-Hop* - 2018
- *Young Grandmothers Club* – 2018

CANDY STROTHER DEVORE MITCHELL

CHAPTER FOURTEEN

DE'MIA WILKENS-ROSEBAUGH

A FIRST GENERATION COLLEGE STUDENT, a licensed life coach, and foster parent, De'Mia Rosebaugh earned a bachelor's degree from National University in psychology. Born to parents, Beorge and Martha Wilkens – from New Orleans, Louisiana – De'Mia is married to her husband Jason for over twenty and celebrates their relationship.

Mrs. Wilkens-Rosebaugh is a mother of three children and has raised multiple foster children with the help of her own mother who taught De"Mia to love unconditionally. She has dedicated thirty years of her life helping children and families who live in poverty or have been impacted by drugs, abuse, and trauma.

CANDY STROTHER DEVORE MITCHELL

CANDY STROTHER DEVORE MITCHELL

CHAPTER FIFTEEN

BONNIE WILLIAMS

CANDY STROTHER DEVORE MITCHELL

BEAUTIFUL BONNIE WILLIAMS IS WHAT I call her because she shines beauty from inside and out. Bonnie Williams my cousin. It is such an honor to be related to such a Queen. I am so proud to share DNA with an amazing lady such as Bonnie who has accomplished so much positivity in her lifetime. Through my mother, I am related to Bonnie; and her and I are also related through our blood cousin Carlton T. Strother. Bonnie Williams's mother is a Strother – I am honored to say this makes Bonnie my 4th cousin.

My beautiful cousin Bonnie Williams grew up in Los Angeles. She met her husband, Stanley "Tookie" Williams in 1981. Together they had three lovely children. Stanley was born 29th of December 1953 in New Orleans Louisiana. He passed away, 13th of December 2005.

A notorious American Gangster in South Central Los Angeles, "Tookie" was the Crips Gang Organization creator along with his friend Raymond Washington, and my close friend, I call my son's Godfather, Mr. Michael Conception.

Stanley Williams' mother was a young mother – only seventeen when she gave birth as a single parent. She struggled financially raising Stanley by herself. He and his mother moved to Los Angeles via Greyhound bus in hope to end their struggles and to achieve a better way of life. By the age of six, Stanley started wandering the neighborhoods of Los Angeles by himself. He grew up while taking a liking to the streets. He started enjoying hanging in the streets more than staying at home. He quickly learned at an incredibly young age he needed to protect himself from bullies in the neighborhood because the streets aren't always friendly.

Stanley "Tookie" Williams is a hero to the African American community, Hispanics & Native Americans. Like many minorities, Stanley is believed to have been framed and falsely accused by racist corrupt police of crimes he did not commit. He was well known and held a strong influence on youth who honored him. He was unjustly convicted of murder in Los Angeles courts and sentenced to death. Like many people of color, he was wrongly convicted of those crimes. He always declared he was not guilty even though he was executed in 2005.

Stanley dedicated his life to God and spoke against gangs and violence. He preached peace. He authored books dedicated to teaching children to not be violent, titled: *Tookie Speaks Against Gang*

Violence. Sadly, despite protests from the National Association for the Advancement of Colored People (NAACP) Governor Arnold Schwarzenegger a known racist himself, ordered the execution to proceed by lethal injection. On 13 December 2005, at San Quentin prison in California, my cousin Bonnie's husband passed.

Stanley "Tookie" Williams was nominated five times for a Nobel Peace Prize. He was a true hero and I pray that God blesses my cousin Mrs. Bonnie Williams, and that God also blesses her husband's soul.

To the Honorable Stanley "Tookie" Williams, a true King to many, I say rest in peace.

ABOUT THE AUTHOR

CANDY STROTHER DEVORE MITCHELL

CANDY STROTHER DEVORE MITCHELL

THE NIECE OF OPHELIA DEVORE-MITCHELL, Candy Strother DeVore-Mitchell, wears many hats. Presently, her newest involves 1) music production company of the *Faces of Rap Mothers Enterprise Artist Members* and 2) television network owner of the *Faces of Rap Mothers Television Network*. These new performance verticals are subsidiary in nature to the overarching *Faces of Rap Mothers* (a California corporation) doing business as *Faces of Rap Mothers Enterprise*. Alongside this – she is also a wife and mother and an actress, author, and executive producer. As CEO of *Black Cash Records,* two of Candy's children, namely HONEY and KING THA RAPPER, are rap / hip-hop entertainers.

Residing in Los Angeles with her children and husband, Candy Strother DeVore-Mitchell continues additional book releases among her multi-series books.

Her website at www.facesofrapmothers.com is undergoing reconstruction and is soon to be released in conjunction with the holiday season. Candy's books are located there and at her publisher's website at www.donnaink.shop.

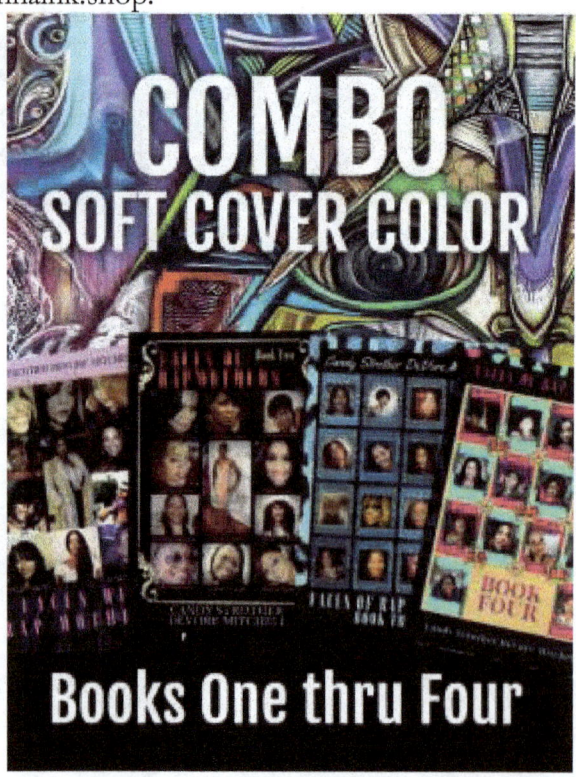

SOCIAL MEDIA

AND WEBSITES

Faces of Rap Mothers Enterprise Website
https://www.facesofrapmothers.com

Beat Deep Books | DonnaInk Publications Website
https://www.donnaink.net – wholesale discounts

Facebook Fan Pages
https://www.facebook.com/facesofrapmothers
https://www.facebook.com/facesofrapmothersmusicgroup
https://www.facebook.com/facesofrapmotherstelevisionnetwork

Instagram
https://www.instagram.com/facesofrapmothers

Pinterest
https://www.pinterest.com/facesofrapmothers

Soundcloud
https://www.soundcloud.com/facesofrapmothers

Twitter
https://www.twitter.com/facesofrapmothers

YouTube
https://www.youtube.com/facesofrapmothers

ABOUT THE PUBLISHER

DONNAINK PUBLICATIONS, L.L.C.

DONNA**INK PUBLICATIONS, L.L.C. IS A SMALL**, woman-owned, traditional, and "Indie" publishing house with thirty plus authors who arrive from nine countries and five continents to share diverse and eclectic works discriminating readers, derived largely from organic and direct sales growth, love.

Top-ten niche' market bestsellers feature quality representation and presentation. DonnaInk Publications supports copyright in a perceptive ethos inspiring written word innovation while nurturing unique vision and promoting free speech.

We appreciate authorized edition purchases of authors' works and for copyright law compliance; in so doing, readers support writers and publishers' capabilities to publish books every reader enjoys.

This year's motto: Love and Peace in 2021.

Head office in Raleigh area of NC.
Secondary office address in McLean VA.
Satellite office in Southern Maryland.

ABOUT THE IMPRINT

BEAT DEEP BOOKS

*Donna*Ink Publications, L.L.C. | *Beat Deep Books Copyright Protected*

CANDY STROTHER DEVORE MITCHELL

BEAT DEEP BOOKS IS AN IMPRINT OF DonnaInk Publications, L.L.C. and features entertainment and media works from a variety of authors including Candy Strother DeVore-Mitchell. New works are in production by additional authors within this genre shelf. All our Imprints support one another regarding specific genres where quality layout, design, production, and writing come together to result in enjoyable reading for diverse readers.

Subsequent arts and entertainment titles are indicative of actor, arts, author, book, philanthropists, politics, radio, music, news, writers, etc. who share the commonality of bringing unique life skills to a creative pinnacle where observers are educated, engaged, enthralled, or envisioned . . .

It is our hope as readers the Deep Beat Books Imprint of DonnaInk Publications, L.L.C. brings enjoyment, a smile, and informative reflection to each of you. Enjoy the journey.

DonnaInk Publications, L.L.C. | Beat Deep Books Copyright Protected

ABOUT THE GHOSTWRITER
MS. DONNA L. QUESINBERRY

Ms. Donna L. Quesinberry (often referred to as "Q") is a small, woman-owned, publisher who provides services through traditional platforms with ghostwriting support for select clients. Ms. Quesinberry captures authors' voices through synergistic collaboration over question-and-answer dialogue. She discovers many facets of a writ through research and study, which evolves into the written word. When performing developmental editing, a thorough in-depth review of the entire manuscript is conducted, from words and sentences to overall composition and layout and design, where applicable plot and characterization is also reviewed and developed further.

Donna provides coaching to her authors regarding brand and image management, book events, marketing and promotions for their works and associative outcroppings with multiple business tracks including DonnaInk Publications, L.L.C. as Founder and President. Her traditional / Indie publishing initiative supports authors and readers alike achieving quality publications discriminating readers are entertained by. She also is Founder and CEO of dpInk Ltd. Liability.

Donna earned accreditation to accommodate a dual Bachelor of Arts in business administration and Bachelor of Sciences in computer science with a Certificate of International Affairs focused on Eastern Europe and the Middle East. She earned one-fourth of her master's before her studies interrupted. She is educated in theology at 500 hrs. mostly as a Sunday School teacher. She has broadcast live and taped on CNBC and varied podcasts, streaming radio, etc.

Ms. Quesinberry is president of *Faces of Rap Mothers Television Network*; she is the chief operations officer (COO) and chief financial officer (CFO) of *Faces of Rap Mothers Enterprise* (California corporation); she is executive director / producer of the DonnaInk Productions Channel on *Faces of Rap Mothers Network;* and a rap mother.

As a published author herself, she features over five titles in print, with another suite in production, and has ghostwritten (with and without credit) over twenty-five business books. As a credited editor, desktop publisher, proofreader, and publisher, Ms. Quesinberry has produced well over one-hundred and fifty fiction, and non-fiction, titles, magazines, and other publications. She worked on *Eisenhower and Civil Rights, NATO at Fifty, An Introduction to Enterprise Architecture*, and other well-respected books including university textbooks, etc. And, she is a recognized poet having published next to Larry Jaffe and Billie Stoneking Marshall.

As a single mother, she raised five successful adult children and is a grand-mere' to eleven wee sprites. Currently, Ms. Quesinberry is a tri-state resident with her son a traumatic brain injury (TBI) survivor and their two long-haired chihuahuas Scuttle and Charlotte.

Visit: www.donnaink.shop for more information.

Follow Me Here...

@donnaink

@donnainkpublications

@donnainkpublicatations

@facesofrapmothers

@3036530

@donnaink

MERCHANDISE
AND GIFTS

FACES OF RAP MOTHERS – BOOK FOUR

www.facesofrapmothers.com

www.facesofrapmothers.com

FACES OF RAP MOTHERS
by
Candy Strother DeVore Mitchell
FACES OF RAP MOTHERS
www.facesofrapmothes.com

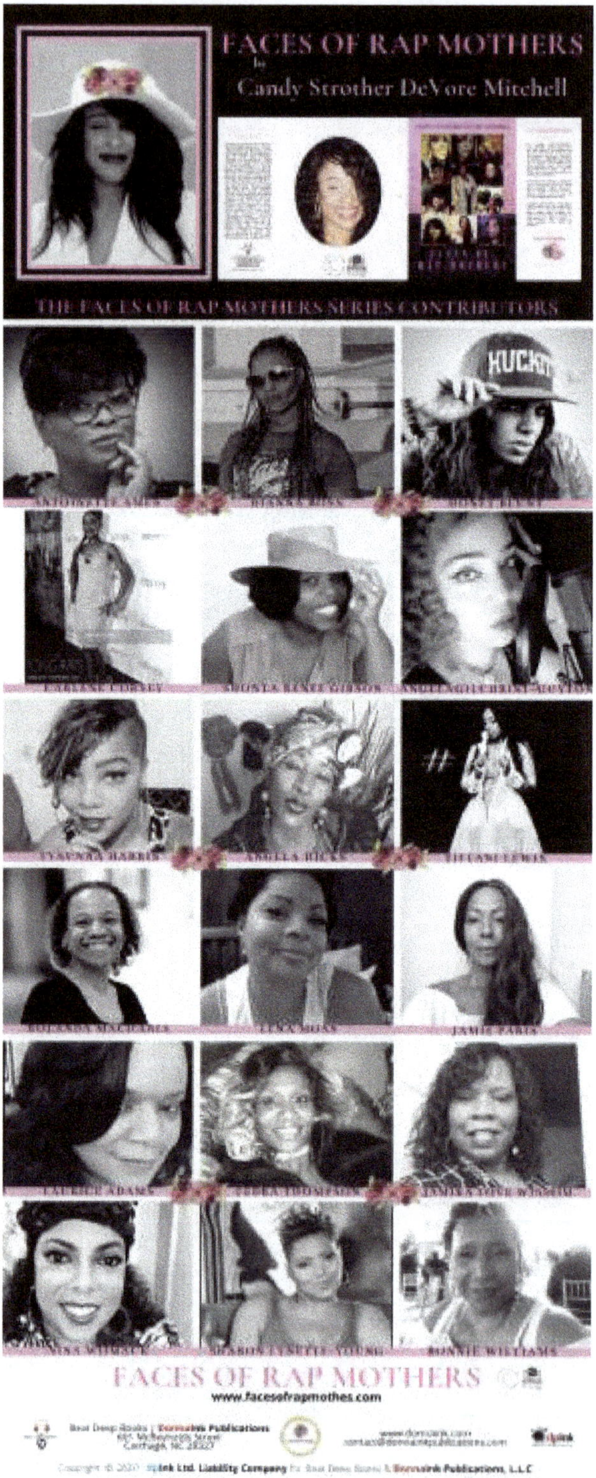

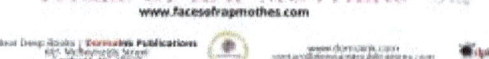

Gimme My

Beat Deep Books
DonnaInk Publications, L.L.C.
17611 Aquasco Road
Brandywine, MD 20613
or
1390 Chain Bridge Road
#10122
McLean, VA 22101
www.donnaink.shop | www.donnalquesinberry.com | www.donnaink.net
www.facesofrapmothers.com
(910) 528-4347 | (301) 888-2414

Email: contact@donnainkpublications.com

www.ingramcontent.com/pod-product-compliance
Lightning Source LLC
Chambersburg PA
CBHW071111160426
43196CB00013B/2539